D0362746

Studying Abroad

Essex County Council

3013020251315 5

Studying Abroad:
A guide for UK students

Cerys Evans

Studying Abroad: A Guide for UK Students

This first edition published in 2012 by Trotman Publishing, a division of Crimson Publishing Ltd., Westminster House, Kew Road, Richmond, Surrey TW9 2ND

© Trotman Publishing 2012

Author Cerys Evans

Designed by Andy Prior

British Library Cataloguing in Publication Data
A catalogue record for this book is available from the British Library

ISBN 978 1 84455 460 7

All rights reserved. No part of this publication may be reproduced, stored in a retrieval system or transmitted in any form or by any means, electronic and mechanical, photocopying, recording or otherwise without prior permission of Trotman Publishing.

Typeset by IDSUK (DataConnection) Ltd

Printed and bound in the UK by Ashford Colour Press, Gosport, Hants

Acknowledgements

This book would not have been possible without the help of UK students at universities across the world who were happy to share their stories. Many got involved in order to share their experience of a life-changing opportunity.

Particular thanks go to Mark Huntington (A Star Future) who generously gave his time and used his contacts to facilitate a number of the student profiles. I would also like to show my appreciation to staff at the various organisations and universities who took the time to talk to me and who put me in touch with their students.

Finally, Matt, Alice and Oscar deserve my heartfelt thanks for their understanding and support.

Contents

Contents

Contents

Contents

Introduction

Britain has had a long tradition of welcoming international students to its universities, yet far fewer UK students venture overseas to study. All that is changing and there has never been so much interest in the possibility of studying abroad.

The three-fold increase in tuition fees in England from 2012 is leading young people to look for alternative, affordable ways to study. Many students are unaware of the degrees available to them overseas, taught in English and at a range of prices. Students from Wales and Northern Ireland will also be able to find comparably priced, and sometimes cheaper, opportunities than those available at home. Scottish students can find free courses available elsewhere in Europe, at undergraduate and even at postgraduate level.

But price alone is not enough to drive people to study overseas. A more competitive marketplace for graduate employment is leading students to make themselves more attractive to potential employers and studying overseas provides the opportunity to produce a more dynamic CV.

However, choosing to study overseas is not a decision that should be made lightly. There are many aspects to consider and many questions to ask before you get to that stage. Higher education is a global market and, although there is a lot of information available online, the challenge is making sense of it, ensuring it is genuine and being able to make meaningful comparisons between the different options available.

This book will help you to determine whether studying a degree abroad is the right option for you. It will tackle the costs, risks and benefits of studying abroad. It will enable you to compare the merits of different countries and their education systems. You can read about the trials and the tribulations of a variety of students, as well as learning about their highlights of overseas study. The book will help you to navigate the plethora of information available, guiding you through the decision-making process by providing answers to the essential questions.

This book is only the starting point of what could be a life-changing educational and cultural adventure.

Note

Throughout the book, you will find terms highlighted in bold. These terms are explained in the glossary at the end of the book. The glossary will help you get to grips with terms related to studying abroad.

The following exchange rates were used throughout the book (sourced in November 2011).

- £1 to €1.16 (Euro)
- £1 to $1.55 (US Dollar)
- £1 to C$1.62 (Canadian Dollar)
- £1 to A$1.59 (Australian Dollar)
- £1 to NZ$2.09 (New Zealand Dollar)
- £1 to DKK 8.64 (Danish Krone)
- £1 to CZK 29.86 (Czech Koruna)

- £1 to NOK 9.09 (Norwegian Krone)
- £1 to SEK 10.74 (Swedish Krona)
- £1 to S$2.03 (Singapore Dollar)
- £1 to HK$12.08 (Hong Kong Dollar)
- £1 to ¥9.85 (Chinese Yuan Renminbi)
- £1 to JPY 119.92 (Japanese Yen)
- £1 to ZAR13.32 (South African Rand)
- £1 to MYR 4.93 (Malaysian Ringgit)
- £1 to SAR 5.81 (Saudi Riyal)

Chapter 1

Why study abroad?

UK students don't traditionally study abroad. Far more international students come to the UK than leave its shores to study. International study might be a new thing for UK students, but across much of the world it is far more common. In fact, the number of international students around the world just keeps growing, with figures from the United Nations Educational, Scientific and Cultural Organisation's (**UNESCO**) Institute for Statistics revealing an annual increase of 12% to 3.43 million in 2009. This shows a rise in numbers of over 75% since 2000.

It is hard to come by reliable figures for the number of UK students studying abroad, but the Organisation for Economic Co-operation and Development (**OECD**) estimates around 22, 405 UK students were enrolled at overseas **tertiary** institutions during 2006/2007. This was just 1.9% of the total number enrolled in the UK at the time and a miniscule proportion of the total numbers of students studying internationally. The figures have almost certainly increased since then, with far more interest being expressed in degrees abroad in recent years. The figures for 2012 look set to climb.

If you mention studying abroad, a common response is that we already have a world-class university system, so why look elsewhere? But UK students are starting to look elsewhere, and in increasing numbers. So what are the benefits of moving country to go to university? There are plenty of reasons why study abroad might be beneficial; maybe you want to avoid higher tuition fees, to have an amazing adventure or to gain a place at one of the top universities in the world.

There has been a flurry of interest in overseas study since the announcement of the fees increases. Studying abroad may be a hot topic, but is that enough of a reason to set sail for foreign shores? I don't think so. Things are changing so fast that it is hard to know what the economic, employment or educational landscape will look like in a year or two, while you might only be part-way through your overseas degree. So it makes sense to consider overseas study in far more depth as part of your wider and longer-term plans; you will need to look carefully at the pros and cons before you make your decision.

The global market

As you walk around schools and colleges in other European countries, it is normal to see international opportunities on the notice boards; summer schools, study exchanges and overseas degrees are far more commonplace than in the UK. Young people in many other countries have come to expect international experiences.

Picture yourself having finished university and ready to look for work. If you consider the global marketplace for jobs, then you will not only be competing against UK graduates, but against the brightest and best from across the world. Many organisations now do business or seek clients in more than one country, so job applicants with international experience, and the increased cultural awareness that brings, have added value. Those graduates who have spent a summer school in the States, an exchange to Sweden as part of their first degree followed by postgraduate study in Malaysia, already have a head start.

Some decide to study abroad as the first step towards an international career. Carl Gilleard, the Chief Executive of the Association of Graduate Recruiters, talks in *Graduate Market Trends* (Spring 2011) about 'the global graduate':

> 66 The concept is becoming very important now. I don't think as a nation we are doing enough to develop our graduates for the global economy. The reasons are partly historic – we simply never 'needed' to; however things are now very different.
>
> Research shows that there is an increase in the number of school leavers going abroad for first degree study. The 'global graduate' is something to be taken seriously, and not just to be seen as a 'trendy' venture. 99
>
> *(Papadatou, A, Graduate Recruitment 2011, Carl Gilleard: The revolutionary road.* Graduate Market Trends *[Online], Spring 2011, pages 4–6 [Accessed 18 November 2011]. Available from www.zmags.com.)*

Studying abroad can not only give you the opportunity to study in a new country, but also to choose a degree with an international focus while studying alongside a group of students from across the world. Consider how all these aspects can help you to prepare for the international job market and the global economy.

> 66 I feel I am having a much more international experience here than I ever would have had in England. I am studying in a diverse environment which is

reflected in the debates and classes that we take part in. My
class has such a range of nationalities that makes the
lessons more dynamic, but it also has a real effect on
personal development. By being in these classes you
develop a more tolerant attitude and change your outlook
completely on some things. **99**

> *Clare Higgins, The Hague University of*
> *Applied Sciences, the Netherlands*

Competition in the UK

Competition for university places

For the past two years, over 200,000 students have applied for
university in the UK without gaining a place. For some of the
most competitive courses in the UK, there are tens of applications
per place. You have to be truly exceptional, and perhaps a little
bit lucky, to get a place for medicine or veterinary science in the
UK. Yet there are internationally recognised universities offering
the same opportunities in the Caribbean and parts of Europe.
Although you still need to demonstrate academic excellence
and the right aptitude and attitude, the level of competition for
places is not as extreme as in the UK. It is not surprising that
applicants, frustrated by the limits in the UK, are looking for
alternatives.

The UK operates a highly competitive system, where great
importance is placed on predicted grades and high academic
achievement. Competition for places is one of the reasons why
entry criteria are shooting through the roof. A cap on the
number of places available means that demand is currently
outstripping supply, so the universities can pick and choose their
candidates and ask for higher and higher requirements.

Other countries do things differently. Some countries will accept you provided you have achieved three A levels (or equivalent) but are not so concerned about grades. This doesn't mean that they are less stringent in their entry processes; in some cases, they are more concerned with how you actually perform at university – if you don't achieve in your first year, they may ask you to leave.

A number of countries don't have a co-ordinated central application process like UCAS. On the down side, this may mean having to complete more application forms. On the positive side, it also means that you aren't limited to the number of applications you make, which can keep your options open. You can even apply through UCAS at the same time as applying to overseas universities; all the while gathering the information you need to decide which option suits you best.

Competition for jobs

Many current students and recent graduates understand all too clearly the effects of the upsurge in numbers in higher education over the past decade. The increase in numbers of graduates, exacerbated by the recent economic challenges, is creating a crowded graduate job market. Yet the more graduates there are, the more pressure there is to get a degree in order to compete. A degree has become essential yet, conversely, a degree alone is not enough. Students are looking for ways in which to stand out, to make themselves different and to get an edge over the competition. Studying abroad can be a way to achieve all these things.

According to the Association of Graduate Recruiters/ International Network of Graduate Recruitment and Development Associations (AGR/INGRADA) Global Graduate Survey 2010, the UK had more job applications per vacancy than all five of the other countries taking part, Australia, Canada, the USA, Hong Kong and South Africa.

In the Council for Industry and Higher Education CIHE report from 2008 *(Global Horizons and the Role of Employers)*, the need for an international outlook is emphasised:

> **"** Global businesses are increasingly recruiting globally. Graduates who have international experience are highly employable because they have demonstrated that they have drive, resilience and inter-cultural sensitivities as well as language skills ... If UK graduates are not to be disadvantaged against their internationally more mobile peers, they must appreciate how the recruitment bar has been raised ... They will be disadvantaged in the hunt for the best global jobs unless they can demonstrate a global mindset. **"**
>
> *(Brown, R with W Archer & Dr J Barnes,* Global Horizons and the Role of Employers, *Council for Industry and Higher Education (CIHE), 2008, page 5.)*

Financial benefits

Tuition fees in England are rising to up to £9,000 per year. Welsh students will be expected to pay a contribution of £3,465 per year in 2012 while fees in Northern Ireland (for students from Northern Ireland) will be capped at £3,465. Studying in Scotland remains free for Scottish students, although students from the rest of the UK studying in Scotland will pay fees of up to £9,000 per year.

On top of the increasing fees, repayment options for student loans are also looking less appealing. In England and Wales an interest rate of RPI plus 3% (making a total of 8% at August 2011's rate) will be charged on your loan from day one, with variable rates charged once you graduate, depending on your earnings. The UK is not a cheap place to live at the moment either, with costs of food, energy bills and fuel particularly high. So, in addition to your hefty debts from fees, you might be looking at less reasonable terms on your loan and high costs of living.

Unsurprisingly, students and parents are now wondering whether there might be a more financially attractive proposition elsewhere. There are universities in countries like Sweden, Denmark, Norway and Finland that charge no fees to UK students. Many countries charge less than England, Wales and Northern Ireland – countries like Estonia and Ireland, for example. There are countries with considerably cheaper costs of living (the Czech Republic or Malaysia, for example) or there are universities with generous scholarships and sources of student financial support (for example, the USA and the Netherlands). Graduates from some overseas universities may come home with the ideal situation of no debt (or at least smaller debt), as well as many of the other benefits introduced in this chapter.

Academic benefits

There can be academic benefits to studying abroad, for example the chance to try out a number of subjects before specialising; or how about the opportunity to study new subjects or specialist options not available in the UK? Some countries are world leaders in specific subjects; Australia, for example, is known for its geology and environmental science courses, among others. Other countries offer a different perspective on familiar subjects, like veterinary medicine or history. Or perhaps you relish the opportunity to study a subject in its natural setting, Arctic studies or American literature, for example.

> " One of the best things about studying overseas is learning in a whole new context. You learn about a completely different history from a completely different perspective. It makes you realise how many daft stereotypes there are about Africa and South Africa that are perpetuated by the western media that are utterly inaccurate. "
>
> *Teresa Perez, University of Cape Town, South Africa*

> " You have to take certain subjects, for example a language, a science and an English subject. Coming from the background of the International Baccalaureate, I liked the breadth of study, but it is a good point to note in case you are not interested in other disciplines. "
>
> *Alex Warren, University of British Columbia, Canada*

Studying abroad may give you a more realistic chance of studying at a world-class university or of taking one of the competitive subjects that is becoming increasingly difficult in the UK (see Competition for university places, page 7). Outside the UK, some of the best universities in the world can be more accessible in the grades they expect and in the scholarships they offer. Different countries place different importance on entrance exams, face-to-face interviews, exam results and hobbies and interests. You may find that what is needed by other universities across the world plays to your strengths better than what the UK asks of you.

You will have the chance to experience a different academic environment, with access to different types of campus and university facilities. Some universities offer much smaller classes than in the UK, better tutor contact time or high-profile internships; finding out exactly what is on offer is an important part of your research.

You may even find that the styles of teaching and learning outside the UK suit you better. For example, in Australia teaching is often more informal and lecturers are approachable and accessible; in Denmark, much is made of problem-based learning, while exams are required in all subjects.

Personal benefits

Studying abroad can be a great adventure, broadening your horizons and throwing up new challenges to be faced. It is hardly surprising that so many students come home from time overseas feeling confident, mature and independent. Understanding that there are different ways of doing things can make you more flexible. Learning to cope in an unfamiliar situation reinforces your adaptability and ability to use your initiative. Most universities arrange lots of events to let international students meet one another and get settled in, so your social skills will get some practice too.

> **66** Studying abroad takes you out of your comfort zone and allows you to see things that you will simply be ignorant of if you stay at home. **99**
> *Nick Parish, University of Cape Town, South Africa*

The list of personal benefits goes on and on. Many courses delivered in English attract a wide and varied mix of international students, not just those from English-speaking countries. The chance to make friends from across the world makes you more culturally aware, but also means a wider network of contacts for future life and work.

Even if you are being taught in English, studying in a non-English-speaking country means that you will need to develop your language skills in order to be able to communicate effectively. Most institutions will offer language courses to their students. Language skills can make you more employable; Britain lags behind the rest of Europe with its foreign language skills, so here is another way to make you stand out.

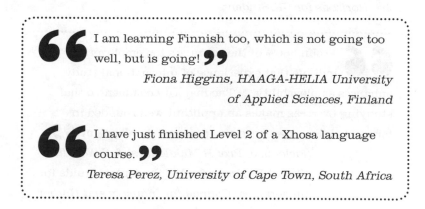

> 66 I am learning Finnish too, which is not going too well, but is going! 99
>
> *Fiona Higgins, HAAGA-HELIA University*
> *of Applied Sciences, Finland*
>
> 66 I have just finished Level 2 of a Xhosa language course. 99
>
> *Teresa Perez, University of Cape Town, South Africa*

Studying in another country can also give you access to lifestyle options that aren't accessible or affordable in the UK. If you fancy a sauna in your apartment building, try Finland. Or how about surfing before lectures in Australia? If you're looking for a great place to ski, parts of the USA or Canada have much to offer.

You might get the chance to work overseas too, perhaps part-time alongside your studies or as part of an internship or placement related to your subject. Essentially, you will get the chance to develop a global perspective or an international outlook, which is so important in today's global society.

The employer view

When considering overseas study as part of a longer-term plan, you need to be sure of your prospects when you return to the UK. So how do organisations that recruit in the UK view overseas study?

The views of over 230 UK employers were surveyed for the Council for Industry and Higher Education (CIHE) 2007 report, *Global Horizons for UK Students*:

> ❝ Around 60% of the country's top employers indicate that experience of international study enhances employability ... The majority commented that studying overseas makes an applicant well-rounded in terms of skills, experience and personal development. ❞
>
> *(Fielden, J, Prof R Middlehurst & S Woodfield, Global Horizons for UK Students: a guide for universities, Council for Industry and Higher Education (CIHE), 2007, page 14.)*

In the same report, a number of large employers gave their views on international experience:

> ❝ The value of [a student's] international experience goes beyond purely the acquisition of language – it lies in the ability to see business and personal issues from other than your own cultural perspective. ❞
>
> *Head of UK Resourcing, PricewaterhouseCoopers*

> ❝ An individual with a track record of different cultures, different working methodologies and different life experiences almost inevitably displays greater cross-cultural sensitivity and greater adaptability which means that recruiting them is lower risk and they make a positive contribution more quickly. ❞
>
> *Senior Vice President, Group HR, Anglo American*

> ❝ The value of any study would depend on what was studied and where and for how long, but most importantly, the value that employers will put on it depends on how the graduates themselves articulate the added value that overseas study has given them. ❞
>
> *Chief Executive, Association of Graduate Recruiters*

> ❝ Given the globalised environment in which we operate, we are looking for people with an international perspective. We are very focused on increasing mobility within our organization as we see this as being an invaluable experience and one which can only benefit our organization and our people in the longer term. ❞
>
> *Managing Director, Corporate Communications,*
> *Morgan Stanley*

If you choose to study overseas, you should develop at least some of the qualities that these organisations are looking for, but you will still need to be sure that you can articulate these strengths to potential employers.

Why not go?

Of course, studying abroad isn't the right choice for everyone and there are a number of reasons why you might not choose to take this option. Some of the reasons that make international study ideal for one person (the chance to have an adventure or take a leap into the unknown, for example) might make it an awful prospect for another.

You do need a certain amount of confidence to take this step. It is a braver move than simply following the crowd and it does have some risks. You are further from home if things go wrong, although many students overseas talk of the support network they build up of university staff, room-mates and fellow students.

The need for thorough preparation and research

Ideally, you need to be fully prepared to take this step. Getting a place through Clearing in the UK can be a stressful process and can lead to students feeling the pressure to accept courses or institutions for which they are not suited. Imagine how it feels when you end up in a different country. In August 2011, there was great interest in late opportunities overseas, but not always the time and space to make an informed decision. A rushed decision doesn't always end up being a negative one, but there are benefits to taking your time with this process.

> **66** The Dutch universities start earlier so I had not even enrolled, had no financial aid or plan, don't speak any Dutch and had no accommodation, so I felt very unprepared. **99**
> *Clare Higgins, The Hague University of Applied Sciences,*
> *the Netherlands*

When considering an unfamiliar education system, you need to find out far more about the type and reputation of an institution, the way you will be taught and assessed, the qualifications you will gain, the grading system and so on; you can't assume anything will be the same as in the UK.

Financial reasons

One of the down sides to overseas study is the lack of UK student financial support you can access. With no loans or grants from the UK government, you will need to find some money for fees and living costs before you go. In fact, if you need to apply for a visa, you will need to provide evidence that you have the money to study. Don't forget to factor in additional costs for application fees, travel, admissions tests, visa applications or insurance, for example.

There may be some opportunities for scholarships and occasionally even grants and loans from your host country. Even if you're lucky enough to get a scholarship or financial support from the country where you study, chances are that you'll need some money to supplement this, or in case of an emergency. If you plan to work to fund your studies, don't bank on getting work right away, particularly if you don't yet speak the language.

Language barrier

If you are studying in a country where English isn't an official language, even though your course may be taught in English, you will still need to manage away from the university. A rental agreement for accommodation or an application for a bank account, for example, will be in another language, so you will need to consider how you might cope. If most of your fellow students don't speak English as a first language, you may feel isolated in social situations.

Learning a new language is likely to be highly beneficial, but it is another commitment on top of your studies. If you are concerned about the language barrier, it is worth finding out how widely English is spoken in your chosen country and whether the institution takes many students from English-speaking countries.

Adjusting

You will need to be prepared to make adjustments if you decide to study abroad.

Education

Teaching and learning can be different (as you'll learn in Chapters 5 to 10). Expectations about what you should achieve in your first year can be very high, often determining whether you are allowed to stay on into the second year. The workload may be heavier than you would expect in the UK and terminology may be unfamiliar. It will be a steep learning curve, so you will need to use your initiative and seek help to avoid falling behind.

Lifestyle

Moving abroad means that your normal way of life will be thrown into disarray. The familiar and comforting will have disappeared, replaced by the new and strange, and the life you expect to lead at university may not always be realised. You may spend a disproportionate amount of time studying, adjusting to the new education system and working (rather than socialising). You may find that other home students from the host country are older or living at home. There will be cultural and social differences to the ways you spend your time and you will be far away from your normal support network of family and friends. In combination, these factors often lead to feelings of culture shock and homesickness. It is quite normal to feel this way, but it is an adjustment that you will need to consider.

> **"** Adjusting has been difficult for me. I have been here for one year and sometimes feel alienated from US culture. **"**
>
> *Simon McCabe, University of Missouri, USA*

Risks

Although many people love their experience of studying abroad, it is not risk free. You might be concerned about whether you will get a visa, have fears about how you will manage financially and worry about the distance from family and friends. International study can bring flexibility, but there may be more restrictions in the choices that you make, particularly if you need a visa. It can be problematic to change institution or course once you start. It is not always possible to change your reason for being in a country, from studying to full-time work, for example, so you need to be fairly sure of your plans before you depart.

No matter how thoroughly you plan and research, you cannot know what you will be faced with when you come to leave university, so you cannot assume that the opportunities of today will still be there tomorrow. You may find that employers do not recognise or understand your degree, even if it is equivalent to those available in the UK. Perhaps you were planning to stay on in a country, but economic conditions made that difficult. Courses that meet certain professional standards today might not fit the bill tomorrow, so it is worth considering a back-up plan, where possible.

> **66** Make sure you research your options for after you finish your studies before you go, I didn't and I regret it. A lot of graduate programmes and entry level jobs in the business, commerce and economics sector are only available to Australian permanent residents and citizens. Also any government related job requires you to be an Australian permanent resident. **99**
>
> *Vicky Otterburn, Murdoch University, Australia*

Finally, international education is big business, so there are people out there trying to make money from bogus institutions, low-quality provision and non-existent accommodation. Be on your guard and use some of the tips and reputable sources of information found in this book.

Having gathered and considered all the information that you need, you may just get the feeling that studying abroad is not the right option for you. If it isn't the right step right now, you don't necessarily need to rule it out for ever. You might want to consider alternatives to taking your full degree abroad (see page 67) or you might choose to study or work abroad at a later stage in life.

Many of the trailblazing students who have already taken the step of taking their full degree overseas have additional reasons for going. Some have already spent some time abroad, have family members who had lived overseas or have personal links to a country before they decide to study there. This is starting to change; as a degree overseas becomes more common, more attractive and more understood, then students will start to make the move without those personal links beforehand.

If you're looking for...

- If you're looking for cheaper fees, try Europe
(see page 96).
- If you're looking for a different lifestyle, try Canada
(see page 179), Australia (see page 198) or New Zealand
(see page 213).
- If you're looking for accelerated degrees or tailor-made
education, try a private university (see page 34).
- If you're looking for a low cost of living, try Eastern
Europe (see page 96), the Baltic States (see page 113),
Malaysia (see page 232) or China (see page 241).

- If you're looking for the best in the world, try the USA (see page 157).
- If you're looking for a different culture, try South Africa (see page 229), Hong Kong or Japan (see page 246).
- If you're looking for no tuition fees try the Nordic countries (see page 110) and parts of Germany (see page 39).
- If you're looking for the opportunity to stay on after study, try Europe (see page 103), Canada (page 192), Australia (page 211) or New Zealand (see page 223).

Rotterdam Business School

Rotterdam Business School, part of Rotterdam University, University of Applied Sciences, offers English-taught bachelor's and master's programmes in international business and management.

Practical Experience

Education at Rotterdam Business School includes a mixture of knowledge accumulation, practical experience and personal development, with periods of work experience and/or study or placement abroad built into the curriculum.

Our English-taught bachelor's programmes include:

- International Business and Management Studies
- International Business and Languages
- Trade Management for Asia

We also offer four English-taught master's programmes:

- Master in Consultancy and Entrepreneurship
- Master in Logistics Management
- Master in Finance and Accounting
- Executive MBA (part-time)

Rotterdam

The dynamic harbour city of Rotterdam offers the perfect location to embark on an international study career.

Both Rotterdam Airport and Schiphol Airport are within easy reach. There are also many options for train, bus, and ferry travel between Rotterdam and the UK.

For more information about our programmes and practical information about tuition fees and housing please contact our Global Recruitment and Student Support team (GR&SS). Tel: +31 (0)10 794 62 50 Email: rbs@hr.nl web: rotterdambusinessschool.nl

Hanze University of Applied Sciences

Come to Hanze University of Applied Sciences (UAS), Groningen, the Netherlands.

Hanze UAS offers English-taught bachelor programmes in a range of disciplines, including: international business, international communication, facility management, fine arts, music and engineering, and offers MBA programmes along with master programmes in international communication, Eurasia business and management, fine arts and music.

The practice-oriented and project-based education system in the Netherlands is world renowned. As an applied sciences university, Hanze UAS is all about preparing you for the competitive workplace of today. You will gain practical skills and theoretical knowledge in an international environment.

Situated in the north of the Netherlands, Groningen has more than 50,000 students out of 190,000 inhabitants. With half the population under 35, and a large international student population, Groningen is known as one of the best cities for studying in the Netherlands. Founded in 1798, Hanze UAS is the oldest university of applied sciences in the Netherlands.

Understanding the importance of building and maintaining strong links with the professional field, Hanze UAS is dedicated to working with industry leaders. During your work placements you are encouraged to make use of this international partner network. Further to this, if you are ambitious and show potential in your field of study, you may have the opportunity to join an honours programme – a challenging route for talented students.

Hanze UAS offers you affordable, quality-driven education with opportunities to establish your international professional network during your studies. See you in Groningen!

Visit www.hanzegroningen.eu

Case study

**Ignas Savickas (Lithuania) International Business
Management Studies**

A graduate of the International Business and Management Studies
bachelor programme at Hanze University of Applied Sciences, Groningen
(Hanze UAS), the Netherlands, Ignas Savickas managed to secure a job in
the UK before even graduating. Offered a job by the company he worked
for during his third-year work placement, Ignas received the offer after
making a solid impression.

'The company liked my strong team skills and appreciated my business
aptitude. After completing my internship I worked hard to foster the
relationship,' said Ignas. 'Before graduating, the company contacted
me and offered me a position. I was really happy that my hard work
paid off.'

International Business and Management Studies (IBMS), offered
by the International Business School at Hanze UAS, is a full-time
undergraduate programme. During the four years of study you will
be introduced to the theory and practice of the international business
environment, complete a study abroad period, a specialisation and
two internships. On graduating you will receive a Bachelor of Business
Administration.

A quick scan of entry-level positions will tell you that employers want
graduates who can offer value from day one. To prepare students
for the realities of the professional field, the IBMS programme
challenges students from the beginning to work in international project
groups. Ignas commented that he liked the adventure of studying in a
foreign country: 'I met people from all over the world and really gained
independence studying abroad.'

Born and raised in Lithuania, Ignas wanted to study abroad for the adventure and chose Hanze UAS on a friend's recommendation. With a job secured in the UK, the adventure continues.

Visit www.hanzegroningen.eu

The Hague University of Applied Sciences (THU)

THE HAGUE
UNIVERSITY OF
APPLIED SCIENCES

The Netherlands has two main types of higher education institutions – research universities and universities of applied sciences. The Hague University of Applied Sciences (THU) is a university of applied sciences with a professionally focused, hands-on approach mixing theory and practice. We will prepare you for the challenges ahead in your specific career. We believe that it is important to tap into the professional world to give our students real life experiences. Our international bachelor's and master's programmes are constantly updated to reflect developments and changes in the working world. Our programmes will encourage you to think independently and explore other people's perspectives, through cross-cultural debate and teamwork.

The Hague University of Applied Sciences has more than 22,000 students and 1,800 staff members who come from over 145 different countries. THU has over 300 partner institutions, all over the globe. The university welcomes exchange students and lecturers from different countries and cultures through the Socrates programme.

We offer nine full-time bachelor's programmes with an international focus:

- European Studies
- Industrial Design Engineering
- International Business and Management Studies
- International Communication Management
- International Financial Management & Control (starts 2012)
- Law
- Process and Food Technology
- Public Management
- Safety and Security Management Studies

For more information please visit our website: www.thehagueuniversity. com

Case study

Philip Rolfe, 26 (Dagenham, UK)

'Unlike many young people, I had no intention of just grasping the first opportunity that presented itself. It actually took me six years before discovering that what I really wanted to do was in the public management sphere. Public Management at THU has everything that interests me: history, science, philosophy, you name it. It certainly keeps you on your toes. The text books create an excellent foundation, and I'm enjoying the lectures which are both absorbing and full of energy.

'The basis we are now receiving gives us lenses through which we can see and compare politics in its various guises in different countries. It's a brilliant programme, really rich and the start of something that's going to be very interesting for me. Another advantage of this programme is that it allows you to work in the commercial sector as well as for the government. With an in-depth knowledge of policy-making processes I could even play an intermediary role, reconciling the interests of business and government, from either side.

'Different nationalities bring so much more to the table. When we're discussing global politics, for example, the input of people from far-flung places is of great value and it forces you to consider aspects you wouldn't otherwise have thought of. By comparison, studying in a single-nationality environment would be a lot duller.

'The university campus is very well designed, smooth running, everything is easy to find, there's plenty to do, it has great facilities and the people are really helpful. And being located right next to the railway station means it's also easy to reach.'

Public Management programme at The Hague University of Applied Sciences prepares you for a career as either a policy maker or manager in an organisation that deals with complex, international public issues – like global warming, trade, peace and security, or human rights, for example.

Chapter 2

What you need to know before you go

It is normal to have concerns and to feel some anxiety about whether studying abroad is the right step for you. As we have already seen in Chapter 1, common worries concern the cost of fees and access to finance; the prospect of leaving family and friends; concerns getting a visa; whether your qualifications will be recognised when you return home; and fear of adjusting to another country, culture or language.

This chapter aims to put your mind at rest by addressing some of the questions you may have about making the move overseas.

Education

Don't assume that education overseas will be just like the UK. There are lots of questions to be asked. When does the academic year start? How long do bachelor's degrees take? How do I know if my university is genuine?

Length of study and academic year

When you start to look at the options for overseas study, it is important to understand that many countries operate a four-year bachelor's degree and a two-year master's degree. When comparing the academic experience and the cost of fees and living, an extra year can make a big difference.

Other countries may also have differences in when their academic year begins and when you can join a course. Many European universities start in early September. Some universities offer more than one start date during the year, which can save you having to wait a full year for the next intake.

Differences in teaching and learning

Education systems vary across the world, so you will encounter some differences when you study in another country. University in the UK requires independent study and critical thinking. In some countries (although less so in Europe and the Western world) university education can be more tutor-led, following set texts. You need to know how education works in your chosen country (and institution, see Different types of institution on page 33) and how you will be taught and assessed. If you study in a country where every course is assessed by means of an exam, you need to be able to cope under exam pressure. Before you apply, you should check whether the style of education suits your style of learning. Finding out what to expect will help you prepare for any differences when you arrive. Your university will be able to tell you more.

> 66 The groups are small and you are expected to contribute, so if you don't know your stuff, it shows. It is hard to get a high grade in essays as the standards are high. However, it does mean that if you work really hard, you reap the benefits and it motivates you to do better. 99
>
> *Teresa Perez, University of Cape Town, South Africa*

> ❝ It feels a little more like school as the classes are
> much smaller and so really forces you to
> concentrate. Also the classes are not the regular one hour
> classes but instead about three hours, but I think it's better
> that way. ❞
>
> *Fiona Higgins, HAAGA-HELIA University of Applied*
> *Sciences, Finland*

> ❝ You have to stick at it hard otherwise you will
> get dropped from your classes and not allowed to
> study. ❞
>
> *Stuart Bramley, Scottsdale Community College, USA*

To prepare yourself and improve your chances of success, find
out as much as you can about what to expect. Read through
the course information and make a start on any recommended
reading before you get there. See the chapters on 'Studying in ...'
for more details.

Different types of institution

Having local knowledge can be reassuring; in the UK, you may
already understand which universities are considered to be
the best, which have strong vocational backgrounds or which
are seen to be weaker. It is much more difficult to make these
comparisons on an international scale and where the education
system is unfamiliar.

As you research your chosen countries, find out about the
different types of institution and how they differ. In Finland,
and a number of other European countries, universities offer

research-based education, while universities of applied science offer work-related education. In the USA, you can choose between university and **community college**. Reputation (but also cost and competitiveness) of the different types of institution may vary.

Although there are only a handful of private institutions with UK degree-awarding powers, it is a different case overseas. The USA has many private providers, and there are plenty to be found across the rest of the world too. Private universities offer a variety of different features; they tend to have higher fees, but often offer more generous scholarships and financial aid. They may offer a more supported or bespoke service, with accelerated programmes, low student–teacher ratio and personalised tuition and internships. Don't rule private universities out on a cost basis alone; in some cases they might end up the better-value option, because of the financial support available and the opportunities to choose a tailor-made education.

University rankings

If you are seeking out a particular type of institution, you might like to compare potential overseas universities to those that you are familiar with in the UK. Use worldwide university rankings to get an idea of how your chosen institutions fare on the world stage and how they compare to institutions that you know from the UK. See Further research on page 292 for more details. Look at which international universities choose to work in partnership with a familiar university back home; it is likely that partner institutions will share some characteristics.

Here in the UK, the national league tables are familiar, but you might not know so much about worldwide rankings. Pay attention to worldwide league tables (Times Higher Education Top 200, QS Top Universities and so on) to check out how your chosen UK university measures up to the global competition. Although British universities are well-perceived, only a handful of them regularly appear at the top of the world rankings. Many universities that we might not recognise as household names are beating UK universities hands down, for example the Swiss Federal Institute of Technology Zurich and University of Pennsylvania are both rated more highly than University College London in the Times Higher Education Top 200 World University Rankings 2011/2012.

UK equivalence

There are two aspects to consider under the equivalence of qualifications. Will your qualifications be accepted by your chosen overseas institution? And, when your studies are over, will a degree from your institution be recognised when you get back to the UK?

The International Baccalaureate and A levels tend to be well-recognised overseas and often meet the entry requirements of international universities. In some cases, they exceed the requirements. In the USA, for example, you may be able to join an **associate degree** at a community college without A levels. You can find out more in the chapter Studying in the USA on page 157.

Other qualifications, like Scottish Highers, or vocational qualifications, like BTEC Diplomas, may need to be verified by one of the centres of academic recognition. Overseas universities don't tend to set their entry requirements using Highers or vocational qualifications, but you shouldn't assume that these qualifications won't be accepted. Each country has its own system of comparing international qualifications to those in the home country. Go to ENIC-NARIC (European Network of Information Centres – National Academic Recognition Centres in the EU) at www.enic-naric.net to find out about academic recognition in the country where you wish to study. For countries that are not listed, try their Ministry for Education.

For all of the countries listed within this book, degrees at undergraduate and postgraduate level taken at accredited universities are equivalent to the level offered in the UK; this means that you should be able to use them to access further study or graduate-level employment on your return to the UK. You will need to do further checks to ensure that your qualifications meet any professional requirements. See Professional recognition on below for more explanation.

Although an honours degree is the norm in England, Wales and Northern Ireland, many countries outside the UK don't offer honours degrees as standard; they might offer an ordinary bachelor's degree instead. Where honours degrees are available, they might require additional work and the preparation of a dissertation. You will need to check whether your degree is classed as an honours degree or not, as this may have a bearing on your future plans, particularly for further study.

A number of the students featured in this book have decided to stay on in their chosen country or move to a new country for further study or work. If you decide to do the same, you may also need to check out how your qualification compares to academic standards in your new country of residence. You can do this through one of the national academic recognition centres (NARIC); for a list of national centres, go to www.enic-naric. net. If your country isn't listed, your overseas university or the Ministry of Education in your chosen country will be able to advise further.

Professional recognition

If you intend to practise a particular profession on your return to the UK, or intend to take further study to fulfil this aim, it is essential that your qualification is accepted, otherwise you will have wasted precious time and money.

If you know that you want to move into a particular field, you should check with the relevant professional organisations in the country where you hope to practise. So, if you want to be a doctor in the UK, you could check with the General Medical Council, while prospective architects should contact the Architects Registration Board.

The National Contact Point for Professional Qualifications in the UK (www.ukncp.org.uk) aids the mobility of professionals across Europe. If you return to the UK with a professional qualification, UKNCP can advise you on regulations in your profession and outline the steps you will need to take before finding employment. They can also link you to the relevant authorities in other countries across Europe. To find professional bodies outside Europe, you should speak to your overseas university's careers service.

The Department for Business, Innovation and Skills has a list of UK professional bodies at www.bis.gov.uk/policies/higher-education/access-to-professions/professional-bodies. These bodies should have clear guidelines on acceptable qualifications. Check before you go and then keep checking as you continue your studies. There is a risk that changes may be made to these guidelines while you are midway through your studies; some students have been affected in this way. Should this happen, there can be options for further study to make up any shortfall in knowledge or expertise.

Quality and reputation

One natural concern for many students is about the quality of the education they will receive overseas. The UK has its own systems for checking quality, but how can you be sure that international universities meet the same stringent standards? When you are making decisions from a distance, how can you be sure that your university even exists, let alone that it is a genuine provider of quality education?

There is money to be made from international students, so you need to be aware of potential scams and of discrepancies between what an institution says it will offer and what it actually delivers. You want to be sure that any money you spend is going towards a good quality education that will deliver what you expect.

Use www.enic-naric.net to find a list of recognised universities from over 50 countries, as well as information on the various education systems. You can verify that your institution is recognised with education authorities or similar government bodies in your chosen country. Bear in mind that if you need to apply for a visa, there may well be a requirement that you are attending a recognised university. You are safer and better protected within an accredited and recognised university.

Ask your university about how it is inspected or checked for quality. Most countries will have national (or regional) organisations making sure that universities meet required standards. You may be able to read their inspection reports online. You can find further information on the quality assurance systems for higher education at www.enic-naric.net.

Using reliable and official websites, such as those included in this book, should help you to find your way to accredited and quality-assured universities. Use common sense when trawling through information and be suspicious of some of the following points:

- a purportedly official website full of errors, adverts or broken links
- an institution offering courses at rock bottom prices

- if entry requirements are much lower than comparable institutions
- if you are being offered the chance to gain a qualification much more quickly than normal.

How to apply

Most countries don't have the equivalent of UCAS, a centralised admissions system, so give yourself time to fill out more than one application. You may have to apply on paper, rather than online, so allow time for the application to be delivered (and take copies, in case it gets lost in the post).

Countries operating centralised applications include Denmark, Finland, the Netherlands, Sweden and (for some courses) Germany.

> ❝ The application process for Bocconi University was relatively simple. I completed the application online and had to send in certain documents. Also, since I did not do the SATs I had to take the Bocconi Admission Test. ❞
>
> *Sema Ali, Bocconi University, Italy*

> ❝ I went onto to the UCT website (www.uct.ac.za), printed off the forms, filled them in and sent them to South Africa. It was a little frustrating that there wasn't an electronic way of applying, but there was very little hassle in dealing with forms. I was in constant contact with the admissions department, who were very helpful, and the university got back to me in good time to tell me that my application was successful. ❞
>
> *Will Perkins, University of Cape Town, South Africa*

There may be entrance exams and additional tests that you need
to sit in order to be considered for a place. These might include
the **Scholastic Assessment Test (SAT)**, Graduate Record Exam
(GRE) or Graduate Australian Medical Schools Admission Test
(GAMSAT). If English is your first language and you will be
studying in English, you are unlikely to be tested on your
English language skills. Check with your institution, or see
Chapters 5 to 10 for more details. Once a place has been offered,
and where fees are payable, you may then need to pay a deposit to
secure your place.

Costs

As we know from the UK, the costs of university education
can change. According to the OECD report, *Education at a
Glance 2011*:

> 66 Reforms over the last decade have seen tuition fees
> introduced in Luxembourg and parts of Germany,
> and significant fee increases in Austria, Italy, Portugal and
> the United Kingdom. Denmark, which previously had no
> tuition fees, adopted tuition fees for non-EU and non-EEA
> international students as of 2006/2007. Similar options are
> being discussed in Finland and Sweden. 99
>
> Education at a Glance 2011, *OECD.*

Note that the changes that have occurred in Denmark and
those being discussed in Finland and Sweden relate to non-EU
students, so shouldn't affect UK citizens.

Finland, Norway, Iceland and Sweden currently charge no fees
to students, either from home or abroad. Within the EU, EU
nationals are treated the same as domestic nationals for fees
purposes, although entitlement to student financial support

for living costs does not have to be included. According to the OECD report, countries like Japan, Korea and Mexico tend to charge the same fees for domestic and international students. Most countries will charge higher fees for international students than for domestic students. This list includes Australia, Canada, Ireland, New Zealand (except on advanced research programmes), the Russian Federation, Turkey and the USA (see Chapter 6 for notable differences in the US system).

> Take out an International Student Identity Card (ISIC, www.isic.org) to enjoy student discounts and benefits across the world.

Fees are not the only consideration. Some countries have high fees, but extensive financial support systems (particularly for those with academic excellence or low-income background). Other countries have high fees but a lower cost of living. Some countries with a generally lower cost of living may still have variations within pricing, perhaps high prices for accommodation, internet access or even alcohol. If you had to pay three or four months' rent to secure accommodation, as you do in some countries, how would it affect your finances? Other costs include visas, travel and costs of application. Consider all these factors when calculating the cost of study and remember that exchange rate fluctuations can have a great impact on any cost calculations.

Paying for your studies

One of the challenges for a student choosing to study overseas is how to fund it. The UK system of loans and grants can only be utilised in the UK. Although the terms of UK student loans are no longer as attractive as they once were, they do solve the problem of having to find the money to pay for tuition fees up front.

Any financial support when studying overseas will need to come
from:

- financial support from the host country
- scholarships
- savings
- earnings.

In most cases, international students have to fund themselves.
Scholarships are often highly competitive. Jobs may be hard to
come by, particularly if you don't yet speak the language, and
some visas may restrict or deny you the opportunity to work. If
you are applying for a visa, you are likely to have to prove you
have the necessary funds; you need to consider how you will fund
yourself before you apply. See page 46 for information on visas.

Even if you are staying in the EU, it is recommended to have
some money saved. Mark Huntington, of A Star Future, advises
young people on overseas study. 'We recommend that even those
who plan to work while abroad should have at least a **semester**'s
worth of living expenses covered before they go.'

Whilst those living costs and tuition fees might not always be
as high as they are in the UK, they still have to be paid for.
International students often use a combination of sources to pay
for their studies: savings or personal loans, income from work
and scholarships.

Financial support from the host country

In EU countries, ask the Ministry of Education or your chosen
institution about any opportunities for grants or other benefits
to students. In the Netherlands and Estonia, for example, there
are study allowances and grants that UK students can access. In
some countries, fees may include a free or discounted travel pass
or free language lessons.

Scholarships

Scholarships are available, although competition can be fierce. You should apply early, often a year in advance, following all instructions to the letter. Bear in mind that many applicants are unsuccessful in gaining scholarships and, even if you are successful, many scholarships do not cover the full costs of study, so consider how you will cover any shortfall.

The Ministry of Education or embassy should have information about government scholarships, while your institution is the best source of information for local sources of funding. See Chapters 5 to 10 for more information. You can also search for scholarships through websites like www.scholarshipportal.eu and www.iefa.org.

Other sources of funding include:

- US-UK Fulbright Commission: www.fulbright.co.uk
- Marie Curie scheme (EU doctoral students): www.ukro. ac.uk/mariecurie/Pages/index.aspx
- Commonwealth Scholarships & Fellowships: www.acu. ac.uk/study_in_the_commonwealth/study
- Erasmus Mundus: http://ec.europa.eu/education/ external-relation-programmes/doc72_en.htm
- UK Research Council: www.rcuk.ac.uk

Charities and trusts

In the UK, a range of charities and trusts offer funding in various amounts. Each has their own eligibility criteria, deadlines and application procedures. If you are already a student, approach your university, which should have a copy of the Grants Register, a worldwide guide to postgraduate funding. If not, try your local careers service or local library.

Career development loans

If you are studying overseas because your course is not available closer to home and you intend to return to the UK or EEA to work after your studies, it may be possible to get a career development loan. Repayments start once you complete your course, regardless of your situation. You can borrow up to £10,000 for up to two years of study, so it may be more appropriate for postgraduate students. For more information, go to www.direct.gov.uk/en/EducationAndLearning/AdultLearning/ FinancialHelpForAdultLearners/CareerDevelopmentLoans/ index.htm.

Life overseas

Whether you will be 100 or 10,000 miles away from home, it is important to know that you will be supported. Finding out the basics before you go can help to ease the adjustment process. Who's going to be there to help you out? What are the essentials you need to know about moving and living overseas?

Support available

The international office at your chosen university is likely to be your first, and probably your best, source of support throughout the process; from when and how to apply for a visa to finding the cheapest place to buy groceries. They should support you throughout the research and application process and will also be there for you once you arrive.

> ❝❝ I got a lot of support from Scottsdale Community College. They helped me with what was on the visa, questions, and everything else in order to get here. Since I have arrived in the States, I have had one-to-one

support from the international student advisor who was fantastic in setting up my schedule and what I was going to study. We have built up a very close relationship, which makes me feel good being so far away from home. **99**

Stuart Bramley, Scottsdale Community College, USA

66 The international centre had me sign up to their mailing list early and sent regular updates on things I should expect and interviews with previous international students with tips and suggestions for places to get furniture, to eat and seek help if required. If your university does have an international centre, check out the website to get some really helpful info. **99**

Simon McCabe, University of Missouri, USA

66 The Sociology Department have been absolutely outstanding since I arrived. The Head of Sociology and all the lecturers are friendly, helpful, approachable and efficient. Anytime I have needed help or an extension or any sort of support, all my lecturers have been accommodating. Their doors are always open and they are always happy to talk to me. **99**

Teresa Perez, University of Cape Town, South Africa

In addition to your international office and your department, making friends with other students makes settling in a lot easier and also provides a source of much-needed support. There are often lots of social activities and events, similar to freshers' week in the UK, to help you meet fellow students from across the world. Try to take the opportunity to meet domestic students as well as international students; local students will give you a different perspective on life and culture in their home country;

they will also have more insight into where to go, where to shop and what not to miss. International friendships are important too and may help to ease your homesickness and culture shock, as you see other people adjusting to their new environment.

> **"** Overall the **orientation** week was informative and there was plenty of assistance in finishing registration. The department has an amazing student association and there are also plenty of chances to get involved in a wide range of activities and fraternities or sororities. **"**
>
> *Clare Higgins, The Hague University of*
> *Applied Sciences, the Netherlands*
>
> **"** There are schemes set up by the university to help adjust to life such as the buddy scheme and family scheme, as well as various trips and networking evenings. **"**
>
> *Warren Mitty, Hong Kong Polytechnic*
> *University, Hong Kong*

There will normally be a team of staff to support you at university; this team might include careers advisers, counsellors and welfare officers. Support will vary from country to country and between institutions. If you have a disability, a learning difficulty or any health problems, you should discuss these with your university before you apply, to ensure that they can adequately support you.

Getting a visa

If you are studying outside Europe, you are likely to need a visa. You can apply for a visa once you have the offer of a place. Use the services of your university to support you through this part of the process; if they recruit lots of international students, they should be experienced at easing people through. They will also understand the reasons why people are declined, so follow their advice. If you can't get this type of support from your university, you should speak to the embassy or high commission.

In many cases, visas are declined because of lack of correct evidence or because of insufficient finances; in other cases, if the immigration office doesn't believe that you are a genuine student and that you intend to return home afterwards. Never lie or falsify information on a visa application; if discovered, your application will be declined and future attempts to apply will be affected. Some health conditions (TB, for example) and key criminal convictions (violent offences or drugs charges, for example) can also affect your chances.

Visa applications can be complex, but it is essential to follow each step to the letter, ensuring you provide all the evidence required.

> ❝ The visa application requires numerous supporting documents, which I had to sort out in good time before applying. They included medical reports, tuberculosis clearance x-rays and proof of sufficient funds. The process of being issued a visa once I had lodged the application was about three weeks. ❞
>
> *William Perkins, University of Cape Town, South Africa*
>
> ❝ Applying for a visa is tedious, anxiety inducing and confusing, at first. You will need to travel to

London and wait for hours at the US Embassy with hundreds of other people. You will need to take part in an interview (which in my case was extremely brief, but I have read horror stories online of problematic utterances leading to further probing). The online website will cause you a headache but if you approach it as just a hurdle to jump you can dismiss a lot of the worry. After you receive your visa you will need it upon entry to the USA and then again for opening accounts etc. After this you should store it carefully. Be aware of things that may impact on it, for example, if you decide to travel or get a job. **99**

Simon McCabe, University of Missouri, USA

Registering within Europe

Although the EU allows its citizens free movement, there may be some red tape to go through when you first move to another European country. In many cases, EU citizens have to register with a local government office. Normally you should do this within the first week or two of arrival. Your university will explain what you need to do.

66 I didn't need to apply for a visa (being an EU student), however to live in Finland you need to get a social security number, and go to the police station to ask for permission to have the right to reside in Finland. At which point you go to the magistrate office (*maistraatti*), apply to have residence and your address is submitted. **99**

Fiona Higgins, HAAGA-HELIA University of Applied Sciences, Finland

> 66 As Norway is not in the EU, they do have some
> checks for European citizens, however, these are
> minimal and it is simply a matter of registering with the
> relevant government departments when you arrive. 99
>
> *John Magee, BI Norwegian Business School, Norway*

EU countries

Austria, Belgium, Bulgaria, Republic of Cyprus, Czech
Republic, Denmark, Estonia, Finland, France, Germany,
Greece, Hungary, Ireland, Italy, Latvia, Lithuania,
Luxembourg, Malta, Netherlands, Poland, Portugal,
Romania, Slovakia, Slovenia, Spain, Sweden, UK.

EEA countries

The EEA is made up of the all the countries in the EU plus
Iceland, Liechtenstein and Norway. Although not within the
EEA, Switzerland offers some rights to EEA citizens.

Accommodation

Safe and acceptable accommodation is essential to enable you to
settle in and start adjusting to life overseas. The good news is
that most universities with international students do their utmost
to place them in suitable housing, often giving them priority. To
enhance your chances of finding accommodation, remember to:

- apply well in advance
- be realistic about the rent you are prepared to pay
- be flexible about where you are prepared to live.

Most students want good-quality, affordable accommodation in a convenient location; you may find that there is not enough to go round, so it is worth considering what you are prepared to compromise on.

Types of student accommodation

If you're counting on university-run halls of residence, you may be surprised; some countries don't offer this option for accommodation. Some universities have campus-based halls run by private companies, while others have no accommodation at all. Alternatives on offer include temporary or short-term accommodation, rental property or homestay with a local host family.

In Helsinki in Finland, for example, one organisation (HOAS) co-ordinates student accommodation across the city and surrounding area, dealing with around 10,000 new tenancy agreements every year. Accommodation through HOAS is available for several years, often for the duration of your course.

> **66** I was put into an all-girls residence; although there are mixed residences. The residence I got into has all single rooms, so I have a room to myself but share a bathroom with five other girls. My floor has a mix of first years and second years. And being in residence allows you to get to know people outside of your course. **99**
> *Cassie Toogood, University of Cape Town, South Africa*

> 66 I am currently staying in one of the dorms, but a lot of people did not get a place. My advice to potential students is to make sure you submit the form as early as possible before the date they tell you. Also, if you do not feel that you filled it out early enough then start to look for apartments. I plan to stay here for a year and then move out into an apartment with some friends. 99
>
> *Sema Ali, Bocconi University, Italy*

> 66 Accommodation can be hard to find, but as long as you are prepared and begin applying early you will find something. The information packs you receive from the university will have details of possible accommodation options. Unfortunately it is not like the UK and the universities do not have their own halls of residence. However, there are student associations who have plenty of independent student halls. 99
>
> *John Magee, BI Norwegian Business School, Norway*

> 66 I live with my boyfriend in a house. We had our stuff shipped from the UK so had to wait a few months for it to arrive so moved in to a furnished house. It is OK but the landlord is crackers. He didn't pay his share of the bills and didn't tell us, so our water was cut off. We are moving out at the end of the month! 99
>
> *Teresa Perez, University of Cape Town, South Africa*

Finding accommodation from the UK

In some university towns there is a shortage of student accommodation, so some international students, particularly late applicants, find themselves in the position of leaving the UK without long-term accommodation. Arranging private accommodation from a distance can be risky. You shouldn't pay a deposit to a private landlord for unseen property.

Seek the advice of your university international or accommodation office on the safest options when finding accommodation from the UK. They might discuss reputable short-term options with you, perhaps bed and breakfast, a local hostel or homestay. Homestay involves living with a local family; it can be a great way to give you time to adjust and help you to learn about life in your chosen country, as well as boosting your language skills. Securing short-term accommodation like this should then give you time to find suitable longer-term accommodation when you get there.

Check what's included

Whichever accommodation option you choose, remember to clarify what will and won't be included in your rent (water, electricity, gas, any kind of local rates, internet) and factor in travel costs; that way you can make a more meaningful comparison between properties. Check whether you will need to buy things like cooking utensils and bedding when you get there.

Practicalities

As you prepare to make the big move, you're going to need to know about the cheapest ways to phone home; how to open a bank account; how to navigate the area by public transport; the system for paying tax on your earnings and much more. Talk to your university international office. You can also ask questions on online message boards for prospective students, some of which are filled with information about accommodation, buying bikes and so on.

Once you arrive, you can start to use the network of friends that you make. This is where the local students, and those who've already studied there for a while, become invaluable. Most people are more than happy to help.

Insurance: health and belongings

It is important to make sure that you and your belongings are adequately insured from the time you leave the UK until your return.

If you are studying within the EEA or Switzerland, take out a European Health Insurance Card or EHIC. It is free and easily obtainable, normally arriving within seven days. It entitles you to the same treatment as a resident of the host country, but doesn't cover additional costs, like ongoing treatment or returning you to the UK in the event of an accident (www.ehic.org.uk).

You will need to take out additional insurance for travel and health to cover you whilst you are away. A number of UK providers offer study abroad insurance policies, including Endsleigh (www.endsleigh.co.uk/Travel/Pages/study-abroad-insurance.aspx) and STA Travel (www.statravel.co.uk/study-abroad-travel-insurance.htm). Alternatively, you could take out a policy in your host country. Your international office should be able to advise you further.

There may be vaccinations or preventive measures, like malaria tablets, that you need to take before you travel. Talk to your GP and see the Travel Health pages of the Foreign and Commonwealth Office (www.fco.gov.uk). You may need to demonstrate that you are fit and well in order to gain a visa; this may involve a medical examination.

"" I'm not usually one for insurance, but as soon as I arrived in Madrid all my luggage got stolen, every item to my name never to be seen again! An expensive lesson to be learnt. **""**

Esme Leyland, IE University, Spain

"" I got insurance from England, a backpackers one as I intended on travelling and it was a perfect cover. I also got health insurance as part of a requirement for my visa. **""**

Angela Minvalla, RMIT University, Australia

"" Health insurance is cheaper than it would be because I am on a student plan, so it's about £30 a month. **""**

Teresa Perez, University of Cape Town, South Africa

"" For health insurance in Europe, you need an EU health card which will cover you for costs at hospitals (up to a certain amount of course). It's extremely easy to get! **""**

Fiona Higgins, HAAGA-HELIA University of Applied Science, Finland

"" I found insurance was a little bit of a hassle as I had to claim for things if I used it, for instance if I went to the doctors I had to pay and then claim back what I spent. **""**

Stuart Bramley, Scottsdale Community College, USA

Personal safety

Although studying abroad is not, in itself, a dangerous activity, visiting different countries carries different risk. The Foreign and Commonwealth Office has useful information for Britons travelling and living overseas, including travel advice by country. Find out about safety and security, health issues, local laws and customs or natural disasters before you go. The Foreign and Commonwealth Office also has a useful travel checklist to follow: see www.fco.gov.uk/en/travel-and-living-abroad/staying-safe/checklist.

Follow the advice of your international office; they have a vested interest in keeping you safe and have an understanding of the risks in the local area. However, you do have to take responsibility for your own safety, much as you would if you were leaving home to study in the UK.

> ❝ I had one instance of crime, but I was in the wrong place at the wrong time, as can happen in any city worldwide. ❞
> *Will Perkins, University of Cape Town, South Africa*

Top tips for staying safe include the following.

- Get to know your local area.
- Don't flash valuables and cash.
- Drink sensibly.
- Don't take unnecessary risks.
- Stay alert.
- Tell people where you are going.
- Keep in contact.

Language and cultural issues

However much you prepare yourself and find out about what to expect, there are going to be some adjustments to make when you move abroad. Differences in language, lifestyle, culture and cuisine may bring unexpected challenges.

> **"** There are a few things that people may find odd or frustrating: the slowness and inconsistency of any governmental organisation you deal with, the general bureaucracy of everything, the fact that someone fills your car up with petrol for you, having to tip people to watch over your car in car parks or on the street, having to deal with mild racism on a regular basis. Those are the things that I think people might find difficult. **"**
>
> *Alex Fitz, University of Cape Town, South Africa*
>
> **"** You would think that being from the UK and going to the USA wouldn't be that big of a shock. You'd be wrong. You will be confused, surprised and shocked on a day to day basis for at least five months. **"**
>
> *Simon McCabe, University of Missouri, USA*

Culture shock is a common side effect of spending time overseas, away from family, friends and the ease of your own culture. It takes time to adjust and you will need to be open-minded and flexible as you get used to the changes a new country brings.

Your university will provide orientation events to help you to adjust and make new friends. Most universities have a range of support services (student welfare staff, counsellors, health professionals and so on) if you find the adjustment process particularly challenging. If you look after yourself, by eating well, taking exercise and sleeping well, you will feel in a stronger position to tackle any challenges.

Other tips to help you deal with culture shock include the following.

- Keep in touch with family and friends back home.
- Get involved with familiar activities, like sports or cultural activities you enjoy.
- Display personal items and mementoes to make your room feel homely.
- Make an effort to meet other international students, who may be feeling like you.
- Get to know students from the host country so you can find out about your new home.

Staying on after study?

After spending three or four years in your host country, you may start to wonder whether you want to return to grey old Britain. So which countries offer the most attractive welcome for students who want to stay on? Canada, Australia and New Zealand give extra points in their immigration system to students who have studied at their universities; this can make it easier to apply to stay on for work or even permanently. In many other countries, working visa and temporary residence systems have been simplified for international students; you may find that you have the right to stay on and work for a period of time, for example.

Other options that can aid integration include opportunities to learn the local language, work permits and internship opportunities. See the 'Studying in ...' chapters for more information on staying on after study.

Returning to the UK

Coming back to the UK after your new experiences is not always as positive as you might anticipate. Reverse culture shock can be an unexpected side effect of spending time away. It can impact on the way you relate to friends and family and affect the way you adjust back to life at home. Try to remember how you managed to adjust to your new life overseas; you may well need to use these same skills to adjust to your return. Don't assume that returning home will be seamless; allow yourself time to come to terms with the changes.

You will need to consider how to highlight the benefits of your experience and how to sell yourself to potential employers (or educational establishments). Think about how you might articulate what you can now offer an employer, what you have learned and the skills you have developed. You can work with your university careers service to prepare for this long before you leave university. Use their support to search for job vacancies and other schemes for graduates or postgraduates. Make sure you get hold of references from teaching staff and from employers; it is much easier to do this before you leave.

There will be some loose ends to tie up before you leave, such as giving notice to your landlord, notifying your utilities suppliers and reclaiming any deposits you have paid. Let your bank know that you are leaving and close your account; this might take a couple of weeks to finalise.

A break in residency?

If you return to the UK having been overseas for several years, this could be considered to be a break in UK residency, which can prevent you accessing certain services like education and benefits on your return. However, if your departure is considered to be temporary and if you maintain strong links or a base in the

UK, your break may be considered a temporary absence. Advice centres like Citizens Advice Bureau (www.citizensadvice.org.uk) will be able to advise further, as this can be a complicated subject with legal implications.

Tax

Whether your absence is considered temporary or not will also affect the tax you will need to pay. If you leave the UK permanently and are not classed as a UK resident, then, on your return, you only pay UK tax on UK income. If you are returning after a temporary period of absence (the more likely scenario if you are only going for the purposes of study), you may have to pay UK tax on some foreign income if you bring it with you to the UK; this doesn't include income from employment but might include income from things like investments. Some countries have treaties preventing the need to pay double tax. This information can be complex and is subject to change, so you should make contact with HM Revenue and Customs at www. hmrc.gov.uk for current information.

You are also likely to be taxed by your host country on any money earned whilst overseas. To find out the rules on tax and whether you should be paying it, talk to your overseas university; they should be able to put you in touch with any specialist advice you need.

Support and networking after you leave

If you want to keep in touch with your wider network of friends from university, you could join an alumni organisation. This should also keep you up to date with events and developments. Other university services may still be available to you after you leave, including careers services.

University of Amsterdam

Cutting-edge research at the crossroads of culture and commerce

A metropolitan university with an excellent reputation for research, the University of Amsterdam (UvA) gives students the chance to study in an international environment for a fair price and enjoy academic, social and cultural opportunities Amsterdam has to offer.

Study programmes for the modern world

The UvA seeks to offer an inspiring international academic environment in which students and staff can develop their talents optimally. It has grown into one of the most comprehensive universities in Europe with some: 30,000 students, 5,000 staff and 300 study programmes, many of which are taught in English.

The wide range of academic programmes means students can tailor their studies to suit their personal ambitions and talents. Not only that, but UvA's international curriculum prepares students for a global career.

Opportunities for innovative research

Over time, the UvA has risen to international prominence as a research university, gaining a solid reputation in both fundamental and socially relevant research. It is a member of the League of European Research Universities and Universitas 21, and maintains intensive contact with leading research universities around the world.

A city of dynamic possibilities

Characterised by a critical, creative and international atmosphere, the UvA has a long tradition of open-mindedness and engagement with social issues, in keeping with the spirit of the city with which it is linked. The tolerant atmosphere found in Amsterdam provides an inviting setting for scientists, entrepreneurs and artists alike.

For more information, visit: www.uva.nl/international

Case study

Ruaridh Hastings (Scotland) Philosophy

'The university is spread throughout the city, so it was a bit of a mission to hunt down all of the different buildings. My own housing is amazing, right in the centre of the city, clean, nice and friendly. There are plenty of computer labs around, although the opening hours could be longer. The internet access at home makes a huge difference though.

'I also found Amsterdam to be a really cool city. It has lived up to all my expectations. For a capital city it has a very small village feel to it and there is a great deal to see and do. Amsterdam is great to be a student in, there is always something going on. I have been to most of the museums in the city now. The cinemas are great. They don't dub the films and Bagels and Beans is a fantastic place to have lunch!'

Flora Farrell (England) French language and culture

'Last year I lived in France and it made me realise I wanted to continue studying French on an academic level. The University of Amsterdam is well renowned and I wanted to study at a university with knowledgeable and enthusiastic lecturers. The fact that the university is all over the city centre appealed to me as well. Being able to study in the heart of a city like Amsterdam seemed like such a great opportunity.

'The structure of classes is conducive to learning. In my programme, we never have more than 10 people per class which makes the classes personal. The teachers all know who you are and you feel valued as a student. It's always clear what work we should be doing for the next week and any queries we had could be brought up in class.'

Maastricht University

Leading in learning

Maastricht University is fast establishing itself as one of the world's best universities, with a reputation as an outstanding centre of teaching and research. Both its prime location and highly competitive fees continue to attract ever-increasing numbers of students from both home and abroad.

Innovator in education

The university has firmly established itself as an international leader in the innovative teaching method of problem-based learning (PBL). In a PBL environment students are personally responsible for their academic education. In small tutorial groups, they analyse problems that are also central to the research carried out at Maastricht University. They conduct discussions, exchange knowledge and formulate their learning goals as a group. From the outset, students have to be active – in this sense Maastricht University prepares its students for professional careers in an academic and a practical sense.

English as the language of choice

Almost all of the bachelor's programmes at Maastricht University are offered in English – unparalleled in continental Europe. Its exceptional capabilities have already earned it numerous international accolades, including amongst others a prestigious Triple Crown accreditation for Economics and Business Administration. It is ranked 109 in the world by QS World University.

With its location in one of the oldest and most beautiful cities in the Netherlands, the university sits at the crossroads of different cultures and in the heart of Europe. Maastricht University is internationally oriented, outward looking and dynamic.

A student-oriented research university, Maastricht University has much to offer the ambitious, motivated student in search of academic excellence.

To plan your visit to Maastricht University or to request a school visit please contact us at info-uk@maastrichtuniversity.nl.

Visit us online at www.maastrichtuniversity.nl

Case study

Dani Older, cultural studies

Dani is 23 years old. In 2009 she decided to leave the UK and head to Europe to experience something a little bit different.

'Since making the decision to come and study in Maastricht I can honestly say I haven't looked back. The standard of teaching has far exceeded my expectations and studying cultural studies in such an international environment is fascinating.

'Within the small tutorial-based learning system they have here you really get a chance to discuss and debate academic questions with your fellow students and the professors. Whilst the high expectations and regular assessments (exams every eight weeks from day one) is tough it also gives you a real sense of achievement.

'For anyone who really wants a unique experience and an academic challenge that really makes you feel like you are getting a top University education I would strongly urge you to consider Maastricht.'

Dani has found part-time work alongside her studies within the University. She is employed to help UK students who are interested in joining her in Maastricht. If you want more information or are thinking about applying for Maastricht contact Dani with any questions on Info-UK@ maastrichtuniversity.nl.

Wageningen University

WAGENINGEN UNIVERSITY
WAGENINGEN UR

Wageningen University: for quality of life!

Wageningen University is one of the leading international universities with courses in the field of healthy food and living environment. Studying at Wageningen University guarantees you premium quality education and an international quality benchmark on your CV. Wageningen University is listed in the top 100 of all universities in the world as published by the Times Higher Education Ranking. Furthermore, it holds a top five position in the worldwide publication index in the field of food, agriculture, plants, animals and environment.

Education

All 28 Master programmes are full time, take two years and are presented in English. Within each Master students can choose between four specialisations to suit their individual choice.

Study themes

- Food
- Economics and Social Sciences
- Technology

- Health
- Earth and Environment
- Agriculture and Nature

Wageningen campus and student facilities

Wageningen University is centrally located in the Netherlands. For all international students there is a room guarantee if you apply before the application deadline. The campus has excellent student facilities; the library is open 14 hours per day, there are multiple student associations and there is a big sport centre where you can practise more than 60 different sports.

Tuition fee

€1,750 per year (EU/EFTA students).

Application deadlines

All Master programmes start in September. Some start in February (see website).

Start September 2012: 1 July 2012.
Start February 2013: 1 December 2012.

Contact

Website: www.wageningenuniversity.eu
Email: study@wur.nl Tel: +31 (0) 317 48 48 48
Facebook: www.facebook.com/wageningenuniversity

Chapter 3
Other options

If you feel that a full degree overseas is not right for you, you need not necessarily rule out all of the benefits of education outside your home country. Whatever the reasons swaying you against taking a full degree abroad, there may be an alternative choice for you to consider.

'I don't feel ready to take my full degree overseas'

Studying for a full degree overseas is a big step, but have you considered taking part of your UK degree course overseas instead? There are a range of schemes offering you the chance to study abroad without always lengthening your degree; some of these choices even bring their own financial benefits.

> **"** I love to travel and I have always wanted to see the world. I chose my university partly based on whether they offered study abroad or exchange opportunities as I knew that I would like to go abroad for part of my degree. I enjoy experiencing new cultures and going to new places, and studying overseas just makes it

> convenient. Instead of taking a gap year and travelling, I
> am getting to travel and study. **99**
>
> *Angela Minvalla, exchange student at RMIT*
> *University, Australia*

As you research UK universities, look into the types of **study
abroad** option they offer. Perhaps you can spend a semester or
a year at one of their partner universities overseas; check out
which courses and in which countries you can study this way.
Perhaps you like the look of a Master of Maths course with a
year in Australia through the University of East Anglia; LLB
Law with a year in China through the University of Kent; or
maybe a BSc in International Management at SOAS with a
year in North Africa or the Middle East. It is important to find
out whether your degree will be lengthened by this experience
and which years of study count towards your final degree
classification.

More and more UK universities now have overseas campuses
offering courses taught in English and mirroring some of the
courses available back in the UK. University of Nottingham has
campuses in China and Malaysia, while Heriot-Watt University
has a campus in Dubai. Middlesex University also has a campus
in the United Arab Emirates, along with one in Mauritius.

What will I pay?

If you are studying overseas for part of your course, you will
often continue to pay tuition fees to your university at home,
rather than your overseas university. If you choose to spend
a year at certain US universities, for example, this may mean
studying at a fraction of the full cost of tuition. If you are
studying a full year overseas, your UK tuition fees should be

reduced to 50% or less; your UK university will be able to tell you more.

> ❝ Once my university had agreed to put my application forward for an exchange, applying to RMIT was the same as applying to university during year 13, where I had to write a personal statement and fill in paperwork, but there were extra things like references, passport copies and my previous year's **academic transcript**. ❞
>
> *Angela Minvalla, exchange student at RMIT*
> *University, Australia*
>
> ❝ Applying for the exchange was very easy and straightforward; it was all online. The staff at the International Affairs Office were quick and very useful. ❞
> *Warren Mitty, exchange student at Hong Kong Polytechnic*
> *University, Hong Kong*

You will still be able to access the normal UK system of grants and loans, with a higher overseas rate of loan for living costs available. In some cases, you may be able to apply for a travel grant to assist with the costs of travel, medical insurance, visas and so on. There may be additional bursaries which you can apply for. Find out more from your UK university or from your national organisation for student finance:

- Student Finance England (www.studentfinance.direct. gov.uk)
- Student Awards Agency for Scotland (www.saas.gov.uk)
- Student Finance Wales (www.studentfinancewales.co.uk)
- Student Finance NI (www.studentfinanceni.co.uk).

> **❝** My university in the UK and RMIT did not offer any financial support; I was not eligible for any of the Australian scholarships and my university simply did not offer a study abroad scholarship. I self-funded the trip with the slight help of the student loan. I did have to get a job to continue out here for my second semester. **❞**
>
> *Angela Minvalla, exchange student at RMIT University, Australia*

If you are studying outside Europe, you are still likely to need a visa in the same way as if you were taking your full degree course; your university will be able to get you started with this process.

With these options, you can gain a degree from a familiar university along with the benefits of international experience, but without so many of the risks. You may get some financial support throughout the process, with the benefit of personal support from both institutions too. It should be reasonably straightforward to transfer any credits achieved internationally back to the UK; your university should have planned for this to happen.

Erasmus

Through the European Union Erasmus scheme, you have the opportunity to study in another European country for between three and 12 months. This is completed as a part of your course, so counts towards your degree.

You will receive an Erasmus grant to put towards the additional costs of studying abroad, but you will still be expected to find your own living costs. According to the British Council, 'On average, over the last three years, UK students have received a grant from the EU of around €375 a month.' Additional one-off funding of €400 has been available this year for those choosing a less visited country – Bulgaria, Croatia, Cyprus, Czech Republic, Estonia, Greece, Hungary, Latvia, Lithuania, Malta, Poland, Romania, Slovakia, Slovenia and Turkey. If you fall into the category of widening participation, there is an extra €500 available.

You will not be expected to pay fees to your host university and shouldn't have to pay more than 50% of your tuition fees back home. In some cases, you might not pay tuition fees at all, although this ruling varies from institution to institution and from year to year. Some universities offer additional bursaries to students opting for an Erasmus placement.

For more information, talk to your UK university's study abroad or international office and go to www.britishcouncil.org/erasmus-about-erasmus.htm.

> The Erasmus Mundus scheme allows students to study joint programmes in multiple countries, some outside the EU, at postgraduate level. Scholarships are available. Find out more at Erasmus Mundus, http://eacea.ec.europa.eu/erasmus_mundus/programme/about_erasmus_mundus_en.php.

English language assistant

Once you have two years' worth of higher education under your belt, you could consider working as an English language assistant. These opportunities are normally open to language students in the UK, giving them the chance to work in an overseas school for a year. In some cases, these opportunities can attract Erasmus funding. This option would lengthen your study by a year, but should give you some valuable experience of education and life overseas. Your university study abroad office should be able to tell you more.

Short-term study overseas

Shorter options to study overseas include summer schools and short placements. You could spend a summer learning a language or testing out international education, to see if you are ready to commit to further study abroad. Check out the costs and visa requirements well in advance of making final arrangements.

Opportunities include:

- Study China: a 17-day programme for existing undergraduate or foundation degree students http://servalan.humanities.manchester.ac.uk/studychina/
- IAESTE: summer placements for full-time HE science, technology and engineering students www.iaeste.org
- pre-university summer schools at US universities like Harvard and Stanford www.fulbright.co.uk
- short-term exchanges in the USA www.educationusa.info/pages/students/research-short.php#.TotkAHLhdQg

'I want to gain a degree from an international university without leaving the UK'

There are a couple of choices if you want to gain an international degree from within the UK; either distance learning or choosing a UK-based overseas university.

Distance learning

Online and distance learning is on the increase. With thousands of international universities offering degrees by distance learning, you need not set a foot out of the house to gain an international education. Of course, you will need to be disciplined and focused, and you won't gain the experience of living in another country, but you may end up with a degree from a top university at a fraction of the cost. It is worth noting that not all universities allow you to complete a full degree by distance education; they might offer blended learning, a combination of distance and face-to-face learning.

The benefits of distance learning are affordability, convenience, flexibility, choice and support (from tutors and classmates). On the other hand, you need to be truly disciplined and aware of the fact that you will lose the face-to-face interaction that you would get on campus. It can be more difficult to assess whether distance learning providers are reliable, without a physical presence to assess them by.

How do I know that my distance learning provider is genuine?

You need to be even more thorough when researching a distance learning provider. See page 37 for some questions to ask of potential institutions. Remember, if it sounds too good to be true, it probably is.

There may be some warning signs to look out for when checking out a distance learning institution's website. If the organisation only provides a PO Box address, if it has a similar name to other well-respected institutions or if you can gain a higher education qualification purely on the basis of previous experience, you might need to dig a bit deeper to ascertain whether it is genuine and accredited.

You may find it easier to be sure of the provenance of your qualifications from a traditional university that happens to offer distance learning courses. Many traditional, accredited universities across the world, and as many as 90% in the USA (according to EducationUSA), offer distance learning provision. If the institution claims to be accredited, double check this with the accrediting organisation. You can find out more at the Ministry of Education of the country you hope to gain your qualification from. Check out these websites too.

- International Council for Open and Distance Education (ICDE)
- Study Portals (search for a distance learning course in Europe) www.studyportals.eu
- Distance Education and Training Council (USA) www. detc.org/search_schools.php

UK-based overseas university

Campuses for a number of overseas universities can be found in the UK, most commonly in London. Many of these are American universities, offering US degrees. Although these universities recruit students from all over the world, only a small percentage currently attend from within the UK. This may change, with the fees hike in parts of the UK now making the fees at these universities appear much more reasonable.

In the case of Richmond, the American International University in London, and American InterContinental University, you can gain a dual degree from the UK and USA, while experiencing an international university and accessing the UK system of loans and grants. With undergraduate fees around the £9,000 mark in 2011/2012, costs are comparable to most of the top UK universities.

International universities with a campus in the UK include the following.

- American InterContinental University
  www.aiuniv.edu/London
- Richmond, American International University
  www.richmond.ac.uk
- Schiller University
  www.schiller.edu/campuses/london-england
- Hult International Business School
  www.hult.edu/en/Campuses/London/About-London/
- Azad University
  www.auox.org.uk/
- Limkokwing University of Technology
  www.limkokwing.net/united_kingdom/

You can find out more about courses, fees and how to apply on their websites.

University of Groningen

400 years of passion and performance

The University of Groningen has a long and rich history and it keeps striving for innovation. We offer over 90 English-taught degree programmes in virtually every field. The university challenges its students to get as much out of their time on campus as possible and it supports them by providing excellent computer and study facilities. In addition, there are great libraries, lots of places to grab a coffee or a bite to eat and keeping in shape is made easy as well: the sports centre of the university offers a varied programme, from Capoeira to spinning and from hockey to squash.

The quality of the academic programmes is high. Lecturers use examples from current affairs in their classes and they are up to date with the latest research. Students are encouraged to think critically about the study material and about what the teachers say. That is why you will often find lively debates in class.

In Groningen, there is always something going on. The city has a population of just under 200,000 (60,000 of whom are students) but it offers a great variety of cultural events, like festivals, concerts, theatre shows, and stand-up comedy. Because of its size, going out for a drink with friends in Groningen is easy because all the pubs and clubs are nearby. Most of its facilities, like restaurants and hairdressers to name just a few, do special deals for students. Everything you need is easy to get to because public transportation is well organised. But it's even easier to travel by bicycle, which is what most Dutch people do, because there are bicycle paths everywhere and it is very safe to ride your bike. Groningen is a safe city anyway: you can go anywhere at any time of day. The atmosphere of the city is always relaxed. It's a typical student city.

While Groningen itself is a great place to be, it has the added bonus of being the perfect location from which to reach many other places in Europe very easily.

Visit our websites: www.groningenlife.eu, www.rug.nl

Case study

Christian Garrard (Canterbury, UK) Second year of LLB International and European Law

'I chose to study abroad as well as in the UK because it is something I always wanted to do. Furthermore, going to the Netherlands would be a particularly useful experience for me since I'm studying international law. Here, I study with international students and gain an amazing international experience. The course I am taking at the University of Groningen is unique: no university in the UK offers a programme like this.

'Before arriving in Groningen, the university put me in touch with an organisation that provides accommodation, similar to the halls in the UK. The application process for my course was very simple and the university supported me in different ways, for example by advising me about my budget. When I got to the city, there were many organisations that introduced me to different aspects of student life in Groningen. There was no problem getting help when I needed it.

'I would definitely recommend students in sixth form to consider going to Groningen to study. You can always apply for both Dutch and British universities at the same time if you are not sure right away. At the moment, there is no financial assistance from the UK, unfortunately, but doing a university degree here in the Netherlands is so much cheaper than back home. In addition, the quality of teaching is just as good if not better than at many universities in the UK. The vast majority of the lecturers have a high level of English, so communication is never a problem either.

'Before coming here, I hadn't exactly known what to expect. The biggest surprise for me was how soon I felt at home.'

Amsterdam University College

Do you have broad interests, do you enjoy discussion and debate, do you like to be challenged, and do you feel at home in an international environment? Then you're warmly invited to join the international AUC student community!

Amsterdam University College (AUC) – a joint institute of the University of Amsterdam and VU University Amsterdam – offers a top-quality, selective, English-taught, international liberal arts and sciences bachelor's programme that crosses the boundaries of languages, cultures and academic disciplines. Discussions start from 'big questions' in science and society and lead to in-depth study in a wide range of disciplines. You can major in the sciences, social sciences or humanities.

As a residential and selective honours college, AUC attracts students from all over the world who study and live together on our brand-new campus. As an AUC student you form part of an engaging academic and social community, which is supported by small class size, a residential campus and a strong international setting, with 50% of the students having an international background.

Would you like to know more? Visit the AUC website: www.auc.nl.

Case study

Nick Tennies Class of 2014

'As I was considering what my next step in life would be and had decided that I wanted to continue my academic career, I knew one thing for certain; I wanted a new city and culture more focused on humanity and the greater good. Amsterdam is where I ended up and I couldn't be more pleased. AUC itself incorporates many of the things I love about its setting here in Amsterdam; diversity, international opportunities, and a general sense of social consciousness.

'AUC's core philosophies encourage multi-faceted problem-solving skills that incorporate a wide variety of disciplines and perspectives. As a science major focused on energy, climate, and sustainability, I believe that this approach is absolutely necessary in facing global issues such as climate change, pollution, and over-population.

'AUC's diverse undergraduate education will help me to expand my horizons for furthering my education in a master's programme and open me up to other passions that I would not have discovered otherwise.'

HU University of Applied Sciences Utrecht

IHU UNIVERSITY OF APPLIED SCIENCES UTRECHT

Study business or marketing in the heart of the Netherlands!

The city of Utrecht combines a rich past and a dynamic present. It is located in the heart of the Netherlands, only 30 minutes from Amsterdam. It is the fourth largest city in the Netherlands with a population of 280,000. With more than 45,000 students, you can feel the academic environment everywhere.

The HU University of Applied Sciences Utrecht is one of the largest educational institutions in the Netherlands, with a wide range of disciplines and professional fields. The international study programmes focus on the combination of theory and practical experience. Students have the opportunity to study abroad for a semester and there are two internships included in all the bachelor's programmes. HU offers you good-quality study programmes for € 1,713 a year!

Bachelor's programmes in English

- International Communication & Media
- International Marketing Management
- International Business & Management Studies
- International Business for Emerging Markets

Master's programmes in English

- Master of Business Studies (MBS) in Innovation in European Business
- European Master in Facility Management and Real Estate

For more information visit our website, www.international.hu.nl.

Chapter 4
Researching your options

There are so many questions to ask about yourself, your chosen country and your chosen university before you even apply. In the early stages, it is even hard to know what those questions should be. If you thought narrowing down your UCAS choices to five was tricky, imagine choosing from the whole world. If that all sounds like too much hard work, consider that somewhere out there may be the perfect course for you at the perfect price; it's got to be worth a little bit of work to find it.

Getting started

With almost the whole world to choose from, the first step should be to research the countries that you are interested in. The chapters on studying in various countries will give you an overview of the different education systems, costs and financial support, how to apply and the visa system. Each chapter will also feature the most useful and reliable websites where you can find out more. This should help you start to compare what is on offer and how it fits in with your plans.

Where to study

This book focuses on opportunities taught in English, so the Republic of Ireland, USA, Canada, Australia and New Zealand

are likely to have the largest choice of courses. Many other
Commonwealth countries use English, including Singapore,
Malaysia and certain Caribbean, Pacific and African nations. Find
out more at the Association of Commonwealth Universities, www.
acu.ac.uk.

In a number of countries where English isn't widely spoken, the
government or the institutions are keen to recruit international
students so offer a high proportion of courses taught in English.
These countries include:

- the Netherlands
- Denmark
- Sweden
- Finland.

According to the OECD, there will be some courses taught in
English available in countries such as:

- France
- Germany
- Belgium (Flemish)
- the Czech Republic
- Hungary
- Iceland
- Japan
- Korea
- Norway
- Poland
- Portugal
- the Slovak Republic
- Switzerland
- Turkey.

The OECD tells us that very few programmes are taught in English in:

- Austria
- Belgium (French)
- Greece
- Italy
- Spain
- Luxembourg
- Brazil
- Chile
- Mexico
- Russia.

However, it is worth noting that even these countries will feature private or international universities with a curriculum in English. Others may well be moving towards recruiting more international students, so watch this space.

How to choose

Many people choose a country for emotional, rather than practical, reasons. Maybe you have always longed to spend time in a particular country or you've fallen in love with a place that you've visited. Perhaps your family or friends have links with an area of the world or you have a boyfriend or girlfriend who lives overseas.

In other cases, the decisions are much more measured and logical. Some have a particular type of course in mind and their decision is driven by the availability of that course. Others have a set of requirements, in terms of prestige, entry requirements or world university rankings.

Others don't even choose a specific country, but make a shortlist of institutions that meet their particular criteria. John Magee, now studying in Norway, took a very structured approach to his search for opportunities across Europe.

> **“** Firstly, the schools had to be ranked on the Financial Times European Business School Rankings, so they were internationally recognisable to future employers. Secondly, the schools had to offer my desired degree, an MSc in International Business/ International Management. Thirdly, a more selfish criterion of being situated in a mountainous country that offered easy access to alpine activities. Lastly, it was preferable if the course offered an exchange semester, to help me secure the maximum amount of international experience. **”**
>
> *John Magee, BI Norwegian Business School, Norway*

In many cases, access to student financial support or scholarships is a deciding factor.

> **“** I found that a lot of the universities I was applying to did not offer the financial support that I could find in the USA. So I don't think there is any shame in noting the importance of financial backing in my choice. **”**
>
> *Simon McCabe, University of Missouri, USA*

It is also worth considering the cost of living, how welcoming the country is to international students (for example, how easy it will be easy to get a visa and whether there are opportunities to gain employment afterwards) and how well your degree will be recognised when you return to the UK.

Essentially, you need to determine what matters to you and what your priorities are. Consider some of the following factors and weigh up how important each one is to you:

- subject availability
- length of study
- professional recognition of qualifications
- university ranking
- type of institution
- size of university
- style of teaching and assessment
- specialist options (for example, internships or specialist subjects available)
- drop-out rates
- pass rates
- destinations of ex-students
- cost of tuition fees
- cost of living
- availability of loans or grants
- availability of scholarships
- opportunities to stay on and work after completion of studies
- interest in specific countries
- opportunity to learn particular languages
- lifestyle factors
- distance from home.

Carefully considering what matters to you, much like John Magee did, helps to focus on the essential and desirable criteria. A final list of criteria might looks something like the following.

- **Essential**: a city centre, research-based university in the Times Higher Education Top 200, offering low cost of living and the possibility of a scholarship.
- **Desirable:** flight time of less than eight hours, opportunity to stay on and work.

Researching the options

There is no wrong or right way to choose where you want to spend the next few years. Just make sure that you discover the realities of life there, not just the pictures from the glossy brochure. It is not unusual to see universities overstating their position to international students, so make sure you look for a secondary source of evidence (particularly if a university is telling you that they are among the best in the world).

Just as in the UK, courses with the same title may be really diverse. You should ask about course content, course structure, how you will be assessed and so on. Ask the universities about additional factors, such as the ratio of students to lecturers, drop-out rates, student success rates, library services and internet access.

If you have the opportunity to visit a country or campus, take it. This can be a great chance to find out more, meet the staff and ask questions. Many students talk about the feeling they get from being on a particular campus and it is hard to 'virtually' recreate this if you have very little contact with the university before making your choices.

There are other ways of finding out more. If a visit isn't possible (and let's face it, it often isn't), try visiting recruitment events in the UK. There are a number of big events that take place in the UK: USA College Day, the Student World Fair, QS World Grad

School Tour, Hot Courses Global Student Fair and the Study Options Expo. At these events, you can meet representatives from universities who are actively seeking UK students. To make best use of these events, find out the exhibitors beforehand, highlight who you want to speak to and take your list of essential questions to ask. Note down or record any responses you get, so you can consider them later.

Online research

Most of the countries interested in attracting international students have their own official websites; you can find these in the 'Studying in ...' chapters. The UK Council for International Student Affairs (UKCISA) has a list of recognised sources of information at www.ukcisa.org.uk/ukstudent/country_contacts. php. For information on European opportunities, start at http:// ec.europa.eu/education/study-in-europe.

All universities looking to attract international students will have their own sites with English content. Many universities have a number of other ways to engage with their potential students via social media like Facebook, Twitter or YouTube, where you can search directly for the universities you are interested in.

Following some key organisations on Facebook or Twitter when you start your research helps to keep you up to date with new developments, events and key deadline dates. You can also attend virtual student fairs (Hobsons Virtual Student Fairs at www. hobsonsevents.com, for example) and web chats from the comfort of your own home. Other sites, like the Student Room (www. thestudentroom.co.uk), have discussions on international study. Bear in mind that information from chat rooms can be useful, but isn't always correct, so you need to double check any facts you get from sources like this.

Who to Like on Facebook?

EducationUSA

US-UK Fulbright Commission

A Star Future for Brits Studying Abroad

Dutch Degrees

Study in Holland

Maastricht Students

Study Options

CUCAS

CampusFrance Paris

New Zealand Educated

Study in Finland

Study in Australia

Study in Estonia

Study in the Czech Republic

Study in Germany

Study in Sweden

Study in Norway

Study in Denmark

Who to Follow on Twitter?

CUCAS

The Student World

astarfuture

Studying Abroad

CampusFrance Paris

Study in Holland

Study in Norway

Study in Sweden

U in the USA

study-in.de

EduIreland

Dutch Degrees

Study in Denmark

New Zealand Educated

StudyInAust

Study in Estonia

There are some great blogs and diaries out there too. Take a look at some of these:

- Third Year Abroad, The Mole Diaries: www. thirdyearabroad.com/before-you-go/the-mole-diaries.html

- Samuel Knight in Groningen: http:// stkstudyinginholland.tumblr.com
- Residence Abroad Blogs (University of Manchester): www.llc.manchester.ac.uk/undergraduate/residence-abroad/blogs
- Maastricht Students: http://maastricht-students.com/ catriona/2011/07/04/21-tips-to-survive-ucm-for-uk-students

Websites like iAgora (www.iagora.com/studies) allow international students to rate their experiences at an institution based on categories for housing, student life, academic, costs and so on. Use this site to get a student perspective on your chosen institution. Perhaps you will decide to rate your experiences too, after your experiences studying overseas.

Many schools, colleges, universities and public libraries have access to Exodus, an international careers information database. The online database features lots of useful information on studying overseas, including country profiles. Ask your UK institution for a username and password.

Students interested in postgraduate study or research should find the Prospects website useful, as it features profiles of over 50 countries (www.prospects.ac.uk/country_profiles.htm).

Using an agent

Some applicants choose to use the service of an agent or an educational consultant to help them navigate the plethora of information out there. Many like the reassurance of working with an organisation that understands the education, application and visa system of a particular country or countries. Check whether you have to pay for the service they provide and what you will get in return. Some organisations charge no fees. It is always worth asking about the affiliations of any organisation; whether they are linked to specific universities, for example.

There are a number of organisations operating in the UK, all offering different types of support and service. Some of these are listed here.

- A Star Future: www.astarfuture.co.uk
- Study Options: www.studyoptions.com
- Degrees Ahead: www.degreesahead.co.uk
- Mayflower Education Consultants: www. mayflowereducation.co.uk
- PFL Education: www.preparationforlife.com
- M & D Europe: www.readmedicine.com
- Pass 4 Soccer Scholarships: www.pass4soccer.com

> ❝ After results day, my teacher recommended that I get in touch with A Star Future because she knew that I would be really interested in their information on clearing places at foreign universities. ❞
>
> *Clare Higgins, The Hague University of Applied Sciences, the Netherlands*

> ❝ I applied through Study Options. They were fantastic and made the process so easy. They copied all of my transcripts for my A level results and sent off passport, results, organised the visa, the course, everything! ❞
>
> *Kadie O'Byrne, Murdoch University, Australia*

Getting a different perspective

Of course, the websites listed here barely scratch the surface of the information out there. The students I spoke to share some great ways to get a different perspective.

> **"** I did some rather intense research, checking out the university website, the city website and the online literature available. I also used more creative methods such as searching for YouTube videos of the campus and the city, listening to the local radio station online and reading the local paper online to try to get a better grip of what my future life might be like. **"**
>
> *Simon McCabe, USA*

> **"** Any expat website is very helpful. **"**
> *Fiona Higgins, HAAGA-HELIA, University of*
> *Applied Sciences, Finland*

> **"** Other people were a really good source of information. Many other people had migrated so I could ask them about which shipping company they had used, how they had found moving and things like that. I could learn from their mistakes and take their advice to make my move easier. **"**
>
> *Teresa Perez, South Africa*

Finalising your choices

Let's recap the steps to finalising your choices.

- Consider your priorities.
- Write a list of essential and desirable criteria.

- Write a list of questions to ask each institution.
- Start to research in more detail.
- If you're struggling, write a pros and cons list.
- Narrow down your choices to a shortlist of five or six.

It is important to contact the university direct, talking to admissions staff as well as course leaders or professors. When you come to apply, this can have the additional benefit of making your name known to the recruiting staff, as well as improving your understanding of what those staff are looking for.

You should clarify the application process, documentation required and the visa requirements, as well as establishing a timescale for the process. The university should then send you the necessary paperwork or a link to the information online.

Try to apply to a number of institutions, while still considering the work required to produce a good-quality application, as well as any associated costs. Applying to a number of institutions gives you a better chance of a selection of offers to choose from.

Hotel Management School Maastricht

Since its foundation in 1950, Hotel Management School Maastricht has acquired an excellent reputation, both in the Netherlands and abroad.

HMSM trains its students to be a manager or entrepreneur in the hospitality industry. Our four-year programme consists of varied theory and practical modules, two internships and the opportunity to take part in an international exchange programme. Our impressive facilities are housed in and around the medieval castle Château Bethlehem. This teaching hotel provides you with a unique learning environment.

Maastricht is an historic city on the River Maas, where you can shop to your heart's content, have fun in the student cafés, enjoy good food and an abundance of culture.

If you intend to follow up on your study after graduating from HMSM, you do not have to leave this beautiful city. You may choose an International Business programme at Maastricht University, or one of several master's degree programmes such as a European Master's degree in Innovative Hospitality Management or a one-year MBA in Hotel and Tourism Management.

80% of graduates from HMSM will find employment immediately upon graduation. Graduates from HMSM are able to work all over the world, in management and consultancy functions.

Would you like to study hospitality management in an inspiring, international environment with a focus on innovation? Do you want to learn the ropes from experienced professionals? Then visit one of our open days (www.hotelschoolmaastricht.nl/opendays) or go to www.hotelschoolmaastricht.nl/application for more information.

HZ University of Applied Sciences

HZ offers a wide range of opportunities and first-class facilities.

A mere five-hour drive from London

HZ University of Applied Sciences is located on the Dutch coast in the south-west of the Netherlands, just a five-hour drive from London.

International university

HZ's bachelor's programmes attract students from all over the world. Next to that, HZ has an extensive network of partner universities, offering students a wide range of exchange programmes on different continents.

Ranking

HZ was acclaimed the best university of applied sciences in *Elsevier* Magazine's annual 'best 2011 study programmes'.

Career-oriented bachelor's programmes

Close contacts are maintained with the professional field by integrating company projects into its bachelor's programmes. Moreover, during the final two years of their study, students gain practical experience by carrying out two work placements.

HZ's international programmes

- International Business & Management Studies
- Vitality & Tourism Management
- Water Management
- Civil Engineering
- Delta Management

- Chemistry
- International Maintenance Management

Admission requirements

To be admitted to one of HZ's international programmes, students must have passed at least two subjects at A level and four subjects at GSCE level.

www.hz.nl

Chapter 5
Studying in Europe

UK students are lucky to have such a diverse range of countries right on their doorstep. Flights to some European cities can be as cheap or as quick as a train journey within the UK. European study brings the benefit of cultural and language differences, without having to travel too far.

One myth about studying in Europe is the need to have brilliant language skills. Increasingly, European universities are offering entire courses in English. Of course, living in a different country will also enable you to immerse yourself in the language, thereby developing new language skills as a bonus. Some universities will offer you the chance to take language lessons alongside your studies.

This chapter focuses on EU (European Union) or EEA (European Economic Area) countries where UK students are charged the same fees as home students. The countries featured offer a range of courses available in English. The European countries that aren't listed in this chapter will still have opportunities for study in English (most European countries do) but you may find that some are more limited, perhaps restricted to private or international institutions.

In the Times Higher Education World University Rankings 2011/2012, a listing of the top 200 universities in the world, you will find universities from many European countries – Switzerland, France, Germany, Ireland, Sweden, Finland, the Netherlands, Belgium, Denmark, Norway, Spain and Austria are all represented.

Compatibility in the education system

Although there are differences in the education systems across Europe, a system known as the **Bologna process** has helped to make higher education more compatible and comparable across much of the continent. With transparent, mutually recognised systems and a clear credit framework, studying across Europe is now much simpler.

The Bologna process covers the European Higher Education Area **(EHEA)**, an area much wider than the EU or EEA. It includes some countries applying for EU membership (Croatia, Montenegro and Turkey, for example) and some post-Soviet states (Armenia, Ukraine and Azerbaijan, for example).

The process of studying for an entire degree abroad is sometimes known as **'diploma mobility'**.

Bachelor's degrees, master's degrees and doctorates in these countries are all comparable in level. The European Credit Transfer System or **ECTS** is used to measure workload and allows comparison between degrees in different countries. This makes it fairly straightforward to study a first degree in one European country and a postgraduate degree in another; some students even move partway through their studies. Credit can be awarded for academic study, relevant placements and research, as long as they are part of the programme of study. Sixty credits equates to one full-time academic year. You may see bachelor's degrees of 180 or 240 credits, for example.

Another benefit of the co-ordinated system is the **diploma supplement,** a detailed transcript used across Europe and the EHEA which outlines any studies you complete and gives full details of the level, content and status of your achievements. It is particularly helpful if you intend to work or study in another country as it provides a recognisable context to any attainments.

The co-ordination of quality assurance standards means that higher education across all these countries has to meet minimum requirements. It is important to note that this doesn't remove the need for thorough research into what you will receive at your European university. You will find a range of different types of opportunity on offer. Just as in the UK, universities across Europe vary in their prestige, research, teaching and facilities. Ensuring that you find a good match to your needs is a key part of the research that you undertake.

It is important to note that most bachelor's degrees outside the UK are not classed as honours degrees as standard; extra study is normally required to gain an honours degree.

Finding a course and institution

When searching for a course, you can use PLOTEUS (Portal on Learning Opportunities throughout the European Space) at http://ec.europa.eu/ploteus/home.jsp?language=en. Try the advanced search on GES Database (www.study-info.eu/index. htm). Another option is to use the Study Portal websites, www.

bachelorsportal.eu, www.mastersportal.eu and www.phdportal.eu, but make sure you select English as the language of instruction. EURAXESS has a database of research opportunities across Europe (http://ec.europa.eu/euraxess).

Different sites often bring up a different range of courses, so it is worth searching more than one site. Although these sites are a good starting point, the information on application deadlines and fees can sometimes be incorrect, so you should turn to the institutions for the latest information; you will be able to clarify any details with them.

ENIC-NARIC (European Network of Information Centres – National Academic Recognition Centres) has information on the education system of 54 countries, within Europe and beyond. The website also lists higher education institutions for each country, so you can be sure that your chosen institution is recognised (www.enic-naric.net).

Entry requirements

Entry requirements vary between countries and between institutions. Similarly, competition for places varies too. Some countries do not have the competitive system we have in the UK, where the cap on numbers means some students won't gain a place, even when they have the academic ability to cope with the course. Many European countries ask that you have completed A level study, without asking for specific grades; they are often more concerned with your performance at university than beforehand, so some students will lose their place after the first year if they cannot cope with the academic demands.

Certain courses in some countries are subject to selective recruitment; look out for the terms *numerus clausus* or *numerus fixus*, which might indicate a competitive system for restricted places. Your nationality should not prevent you from accessing education in any EU country, although you will need to ensure you meet any entry requirements.

What is your UK qualification equivalent to?

Unless you have taken an internationally recognised qualification, like an international baccalaureate, it is possible that your UK qualifications will need to be compared to the qualifications in the country where you wish to study. A levels tend to be understood overseas, but many other UK qualifications will require further evaluation. Each country has their own system for ensuring the adequate comparison of academic qualifications. Your chosen institution will be able to advise you further on any information that they require, so it is best to speak to them initially. You may later need to contact the ENIC-NARIC organisation in your host country for formal comparison of your qualifications (www.enic-naric.net). There will be a fee for this service.

Applying

Each European country has its own system and timescale for application. In some countries this is centralised, a bit like UCAS, but in other cases you have to apply individually to each university. The country guides will give you an idea of the different systems for application.

Registering your stay

Although UK students studying in the EU or the EEA will not require a visa, you will need to register your stay if you are going to be in the country for longer than three months. In most countries, you simply need to take your passport to a police station or immigration department. It is advisable to do this early; in some cases it must be done in the first week. Some countries charge a small fee for this service. Your university international office will be able to tell you more.

Costs and help with finances

For course fees, UK nationals studying in other EU countries are treated in the same way as home students from that particular country. That means that they pay the same fees as home students. Tuition fee loans may also be available to EU students, in the countries where they are offered to home students. This support does not automatically extend to maintenance grants and loans, although some countries choose to offer this to EU students. Your university should be able to tell you more about the possibility of a loan and any conditions you might need to meet.

The Netherlands is one of the few countries offering grants and loans to EU students, although you will need to be in work to access the grants. Loans are also available, but you will need to be aged under 30. For more details, see the country profile for the Netherlands on page 135.

There are public and private universities across the EU and EEA. Public universities are more likely to have a standardised system of tuition fees. In France, for example, courses at public universities tend to cost the same, regardless of subject or institution. In other countries, different courses or universities can charge varying amounts. Private institutions will charge a broader range of fees, often based on what they believe the market (i.e. the student) is prepared to pay. On the other hand, private institutions may well have additional opportunities for scholarships and favourable financial support, so it is worth investigating further.

Cultural differences

Although you may be familiar with some of the European countries on the UK's doorstep, there will still be cultural differences to come to terms with. Different countries and their inhabitants have their own distinctive characteristics that you will need to get used to if you are to adjust properly. Although the language barrier may not impact on your ability to study (when courses are taught in English), it can add to your isolation outside the university environment. Taking advantage of language classes can be an important factor when trying to settle in.

In some countries, many students stay in their local area and part-time study is common, while elsewhere students traditionally go to university when they are older; all this will impact on your university experience, so it is important to look into this before you decide on your venue for study.

> **66** Although Norwegians are proficient in English, they often are still reluctant or embarrassed to speak it unless they have to. This can make the process of getting to know other students slower than in other countries. However, once you get to know them they are great, fun loving and sporty people. **99**
>
> *John Magee, BI Norwegian Business School, Norway*

> **66** The lifestyle is amazing; it's so easy and the social life is ideal for students. But it's not so easy to get a job in Finland if you don't speak Finnish, unless you're alright with doing jobs that don't require the language to start with, like washing dishes. **99**
>
> *Fiona Higgins, HAAGA-HELIA, University of Applied Sciences, Finland*

Talk to your university's international office or try to make contact with other UK students in preparation for the cultural differences you will face.

Working while studying

The opportunities to work will vary from country to country, often based on the number of local job opportunities for those with skills in English. In some countries, your opportunities will be limited so, to be on the safe side, you should plan your finances with the expectation that you will not find work.

If you need to work to get access to student grants and loans, as in the Netherlands, it may be worth moving to your new country a little earlier to begin the search. Alternatively, you can search for job opportunities through the European Job Mobility Portal (EURES) at http://ec.europa.eu/eures/home.jsp?lang=en. Your university may also have job shops advertising student job vacancies.

If you hope to work in Europe, either during or after your studies, it may be useful to prepare a **Europass** CV, which comprises a standard CV template used widely across Europe; it should make your educational background and work experience more easily understood. Find out more at http://europass.cedefop. europa.eu.

Staying on after study

As a free mover in Europe, staying on after study should not be restricted by legislation, although it may be limited by local opportunities. Competence in the local language, economic issues and local job opportunities may determine whether you choose to stay on for further study or work. Even if you don't remain in your university town or country, most students talk about the realisation that there is a whole world of opportunities out there for them.

> **❝** I plan to work for several years before I apply for an MBA, either at the University of Bocconi or at another university in the States. **❞**
>
> *Sema Ali, Italy*

> **❝** I plan on heading to Asia with my degree, hopefully China. Leaving and seeing what it is like to live outside of the UK has confirmed my idea to live away from home. **❞**
>
> *Fiona Higgins, HAAGA-HELIA, University of Applied Sciences, Finland*

Country-specific information

Note

A number of European countries are very limited in the undergraduate courses they offer taught in English at public institutions. The list includes Austria, Belgium, France, Iceland, Italy, Spain and Norway. However, private providers and international universities in these countries do offer a range of undergraduate degrees taught in English; they will be more expensive than the public institutions, but might still end up being cheaper than the UK due to a more generous package of scholarships or financial support.

Belgium

Higher education in Belgium

The Flemish and French communities each have their own education system. Most higher education opportunities in Belgium require Flemish or French language skills, but there are some courses taught in English. These are more often at postgraduate level, with quite limited options for undergraduate study.

Applying

Applications need to be in quite early with most September start courses showing deadlines of mid-September the previous academic year. Apply direct to your chosen university.

Costs

Tuition is free, although there are registration fees which can be quite substantial. See the sample courses below for examples. The cost of living in Belgium is comparable to Denmark and Australia, which makes it slightly more expensive than the UK. It is ranked at number 4 out of 83 countries on the Numbeo 2011 Cost of Living Index at www.numbeo.com.

> Three of Belgium's universities can be found in the Times Higher Education World University Rankings Top 200 for 2011/2012.

Courses

BBA Bachelor of Business Administration
Hogeschool-Universiteit Brussel, Brussels
30 months
Apply by 15 September
Annual fees €567 (£488)
Monthly living costs €750 (£646)

Master's degree in European Journalism
IHECS, Brussels
12 months
Apply by 15 September
Annual fees €900 (£775)
Monthly living costs €700 (£603)

Master's degree in Governance & Development
Universiteit Antwerpen, Antwerp
12 months
Apply by 1 February/1 April/1 September, various start dates
available
Annual fees €1,000 (£862)
Monthly living costs €700 (£603)

Luxembourg could provide an alternative venue to
Belgium, although any opportunities taught in English
are likely to require additional skills in French, German or
Luxembourgish. The only university is the University of
Luxembourg (wwwen.uni.lu), although there are a couple of
international campuses there too. Find out more at ENIC-
NARIC's Luxembourg page, www.enic-naric.net/index.
aspx?c=Luxembourg

www.highereducation.be (Flemish community)
www.studyinbelgium.be (French community)

Cyprus

Higher education in Cyprus
Cypriots understand the value of international education. In
2008/2009,Cyprus sent around 20,000 of its own students
overseas to study. At the same time, around 10,000 international
students were studying on the island.

Higher education in Cyprus is based at universities and non-universities, both public and private. Some institutions offer courses taught in English, although there appear to be more opportunities in the private institutions. There is a separate system in place in Turkish Northern Cyprus, where universities primarily offer courses taught in English; these institutions are not recognised by the Republic of Cyprus. You will be expected to make a direct application and applicants may be required to sit entrance exams.

Bachelor's degrees tend to take four years, with master's degrees taking from one year and doctorates from three to eight years.

Costs

In the public institutions, you can expect tuition fees of around €3,000 per year for bachelor's degrees, €5,000 for master's degrees, followed by €4,000 for doctoral degrees.

Cyprus came 17th out of 83 countries in a 2011 cost of living ranking; it should be very slightly cheaper than the UK and New Zealand (see www.numbeo.com).

Sample courses

BA English Language and Literature
Intercollege, Nicosia (private)
Four years
Apply by 1 October
Annual fees €7,050 (£6,077)
Monthly living costs €500 (£431)

MBA
Cyprus International Institute of Management, Nicosia (private)
One year
Apply at any time to start at any time
Annual fees €15,000 (£12,931)
Monthly living costs €600 (£517)

> If you're looking for higher education on another island, then how about Malta? Find out more at the ENIC-NARIC country page for Malta, www.enic-naric.net/index.aspx?c—alta. Malta only has one university; the website for the University of Malta is at www.um.edu.mt.

www.highereducation.ac.cy/en
www.trncpio.org

Czech Republic

The Czech Republic has a long tradition of higher education and is home to the oldest university in central Europe. It offers a range of courses in English, and low living costs.

Higher education in the Czech Republic

Courses in the Czech Republic are based at public universities and private colleges, some of which are international. They run a two-semester system, with courses starting in September or February. Undergraduate studies tend to take three to four years, with master's degrees taking two to three years and doctorates from three years.

> There are opportunities to study for competitive courses like medicine, dentistry and veterinary science in the Czech Republic and other countries in Eastern Europe.

Applying

Applications are made direct to your chosen university, often before a deadline in the spring. Additional requirements might include academic transcripts and certificates, a **letter of motivation**, an admissions test and interview. Your university international office will advise further on all aspects of the application process.

You can search for courses through the database on Higher
Education Studies at www.naric.cz/HigherDB/index.php?Sezn=S1,
as well as through PLOTEUS and the Study Portals listed on
pages 101–2.

Costs

Although tuition fees for courses taught in Czech are free, you
will be charged fees for courses taught in English. Fees vary
from around €2,000 (£1,724) but can be as much as €14,000
(£12,068) for a degree in medicine or dentistry. Scholarships may
be available; you can find out more at the Ministry of Education,
Youth and Sports (www.msmt.cz) or from your university.

For its cost of living in 2011, the Czech Republic is ranked 49
out of 83 countries according to Numbeo (www.numbeo.com),
which is considerably lower than Western Europe and the Nordic
countries. Study in the Czech Republic (www.studyin.cz) suggests
allowing for living costs of around US$350–US$750 (£225–£483)
per month.

Sample courses

BSc Chemistry and Materials Technology
Tomas Bata University, Zlin
Three years
Apply by 29 May
Annual fees €2,000 (£1,724)
Monthly living costs €200 (£172)

BA (Hons) Fine Art Experimental Media
Prague College, Prague (degrees validated by University of
Teesside)
Three years
Direct application at various dates, depending on chosen start date
Annual fees CZK 99,000 (£3,315)
Monthly living costs not provided

MSc Forestry, Water & Landscape Management

Ceska Zemedelska Univerzita v Praze, Prague

Two years

Apply by June 30

Annual fees €3,200 (£2,758)

Monthly living costs €310 (£267)

If you're interested in opportunities in Eastern Europe, have you considered Bulgaria, Hungary, Poland, Romania, Slovakia or Slovenia? Find out more at:

- ENIC-NARIC country page for Bulgaria, www.enic-naric.net/index.aspx?c=Bulgaria
- Study Hungary, www.studyhungary.hu
- Study in Poland, www.studyinpoland.pl
- ENIC-NARIC country page for Romania, www.enic-naric.net/index.aspx?c=Romania
- Study in Slovakia, www.studyin.sk
- Slovenia, www.slovenia.si/en/study

---

www.studyin.cz

Denmark

Denmark offers over 500 higher education programmes taught in English. Education in Denmark centres on problem-based learning, developing your ability to present creative solutions to complex problems. Denmark has a strong tradition of public universities and, best of all, there are no tuition fees. At PhD level, there are even fully funded, salaried opportunities in English.

Higher education in Denmark

You can study at research universities *(universitet)* at undergraduate and postgraduate level; it takes at least three years to complete a bachelor's degree, two years for a master's and three or four for a doctorate. Programmes at **university colleges** *(professionshøjskole)* are more professional in nature, leading to three- to four-year professional undergraduate degrees in areas like engineering, teaching or business. Academies of professional higher education *(erhvervsakademier)* offer degrees in partnership with universities and two-year academy profession degrees (AP); an AP can be topped up to a professional bachelor's degree with further study.

The academic year runs from September to June, with the possibility of February intake too. Some courses are competitive and have additional requirements beyond the completion of A level-standard qualifications.

Exams are required for all courses in Denmark.

Applying

At undergraduate level, applications can be made through the Danish Co-ordinated Application System (KOT) at www.optagelse.dk/vejledninger/english/index.html. Danish students can apply online but UK students will need to send their forms by post. You can choose up to eight courses and can opt for a quota 1 or quota 2 application; the option you choose depends on the qualification you are applying with – your chosen university will advise you which one is most suitable. Direct application is required at postgraduate level. Application deadlines are usually in March.

Students applying through KOT also have the option to be put on standby; this means being added to a waiting list if you are not admitted initially. If you get a standby offer, you may be contacted about a place as late as two weeks into the semester; if you get a standby offer which doesn't become a study place, you will be guaranteed a place for the following year.

Costs

Danish students are eligible for State Educational Support (SU) in the form of a grant of around €700 (£603) per month and access to loans. In some cases, under Danish rules or under EU law, students from other countries may qualify, particularly if you are classed as a worker in Denmark. For further explanation see the Ministry of Education website, www.su.dk/English/Sider/ equalstatuseurules.aspx. Some scholarships may be available. See Study in Denmark for details.

Denmark is an expensive country to live in. It comes in at number three in the cost of living rankings 2011 (www.numbeo. com), but with no fees and wages of around €12 (£10) per hour for students, it is still possible to have a reasonable standard of living. Students with no Danish language can find opportunities in English-speaking bars and cafés, for example.

Aarhus University (ranked 125), University of Copenhagen (135) and the Technical University of Denmark (178) are all in the Times Higher Education World University Rankings Top 200 for 2011/2012. UK universities with comparable rankings are University of York (121), University of Nottingham (140) and University of Liverpool (181).

Sample courses

Professional Bachelor of Architectural Technology and Construction Management
KEA Copenhagen School of Design and Technology, Copenhagen

Three and a half years
Apply through KOT (by 15 March for September start) or direct
Tuition fees €0
Monthly living costs €650 (£560)

BEng in Mechatronics
Syddansk Universitet (University of Southern Denmark),
Sønderborg
Three and a half years
Apply through KOT
Tuition fees €0
Monthly living costs €650 (£560)

MA Cognitive Semiotics
Aarhus Universitet, Aarhus
Two years
Direct application by 1 March for September start
Tuition fees €0
Monthly living costs €700 (£603)

www.studyindenmark.dk

Estonia

Higher education in Estonia

Estonia offers good value for money and a vibrant student life.
The country is keen to attract international students and is
expanding its courses taught in English; it currently offers
more than 100 recognised degrees taught in English. These
programmes are accredited and are available at the following
institutions:

- Estonian Academy of Arts : www.artun.ee
- Estonian Academy of Music and Theatre :
  www.ema.edu.ee

- Estonian University of Life Sciences: www.emu.ee
- Tallinn University: www.tlu.ee
- Tallinn University of Technology: www.ttu.ee/en
- University of Tartu: www.ut.ee
- Estonian Business School: www.ebs.ee

Other higher education institutions may offer alternative options taught in English, including modules for exchange students or short courses.

Education in Estonia takes place in public universities, private universities and professional higher education institutions. The academic year starts in September and is divided into two semesters. Generally, you would be looking at a three-year academic bachelor's degree, a one- to two-year master's qualification and a three- to four-year doctorate. Programmes in medicine, dentistry, pharmacy, veterinary science, architecture and civil engineering take five to six years.

All courses include exams which take place at the end of each semester. Grades are standardised, ranging from A (or 5) to E (or 1). A grade F (or 0) means that the assessment has not been passed.

Applying

Applications should be made direct to your chosen institution. Deadline dates are set by the individual institutions and range from May to August for courses starting in September. Some doctorates are open to applications all year round.

Costs

According to Study in Estonia, fees range from €1,023 to €7,350 (£881 to £6,336) per year. Medicine, law, business administration and social sciences are often more expensive.

Estonia is one of the few countries offering some form of financial support to EU students.

The Ministry of Education and Research has indicated that EU students can also be considered for study allowances in Estonia: 'Students can also apply for study allowances, but only if they are enrolled to full-time studies in Estonia. The allowance is €55.93 (£48) per month. Allowance is built up on merit, so a student cannot apply for a study allowance in the first semester. Doctoral students with a state-funded study place can apply for an allowance of €383.47 (£330.57) per month.'

Some scholarships are available, primarily for postgraduate study; ask your university for more information.

Livings costs in Estonia are reasonable. Monthly accommodation ranges from €80 to €190 (£68–£137) in dormitories to €100–€510 (£86–£439) in private flats. Estonia is ranked at number 53 out of 83 countries on the cost of living rankings for 2011; this is considerably lower than the UK and much of Western Europe.

Sample courses
Bachelor of Law
Tallinn University of Technology, Tallinn
Three years
Direct application from January to 1 July
Annual tuition fee €2,580 (£2,224)
Monthly living costs €650 (£560)

Master's degree in Baltic Studies
University of Tartu, Tartu
Two years
Possibility to gain dual degree (MA History from West Virginia

University, USA)

Apply direct by 1 June

Annual tuition fee €3,195 (£2,754)

Monthly living costs €400 (£344)

If you're interested in opportunities in the Baltic States, have you considered Latvia and Lithuania? Find out more at Study in Latvia, www.studyinlatvia.lv and Study in Lithuania, www.smpf.lt/en/studyinlt/about_lithuania and the Lithuanian Centre for Quality Assessment in Higher Education, www.skvc.lt/en/content.asp?id=235.

---

www.studyinestonia.ee

Finland

Finland is considered to be a safe and forward-looking nation with a high-quality education system. Temperatures can range from +30°C to -20°C and the sun never sets in parts of the country in June and early July. The academic year runs from August to the end of May; it is split into two semesters, August to December and January to May. Most students start in August, with limited opportunities to join in January.

Higher education in Finland

Higher education in Finland takes places in research-based universities or vocationally focussed **polytechnics** (or **Universities of Applied Sciences**). In the universities, few programmes are taught in English at undergraduate level, although master's and doctoral degrees are more widely available. It is the opposite in the polytechnics, where there are plenty of programmes taught in English at undergraduate level, with a smaller number of UAS master's programmes. (Doctoral qualifications are not available in the polytechnics, only in the universities.) To access a UAS master's programme, you will need to have had three years of relevant experience, in addition to any academic requirements. To search for programmes, go to the Study in Finland database at www.studyinfinland.fi/study_ options/study_programmes_database.

The degrees vary in length as follows:

- bachelor's degree: three years (university); three and a half to four years (polytechnic/university of applied sciences)
- master's degree: two years (university); one and a half to two years (polytechnic/**university of applied sciences**)
- doctoral degree: three to four years (university); not available at polytechnic/university of applied sciences.

Applying

Applications tend to be online, although the application process and timescale are split between the universities and polytechnics.

At universities, undergraduate applications are direct. Applications to master's programmes can be made direct or via www.universityadmissions.fi; ask your university which way to proceed. In most cases, you should apply for bachelor's and master's degrees between November and January. Doctoral programmes require direct application; the application timescale varies between institutions, some accept applications at any time, while others have specific timescales in which to apply. Speak to the international office or the relevant faculty at your chosen university.

At polytechnics, undergraduate applications should be made in January or February via www.admissions.fi. For a UAS master's degree, you should apply directly to the polytechnic at the time they specify; you can find out more on your chosen institution's website.

Undergraduate admissions procedures normally require an entrance test. This tends to be a written test, but may be an audition or portfolio for certain art, drama or music programmes. Most university tests are taken in Finland, but some polytechnic entrance tests can be taken outside the country. Make sure you prepare fully, following any instructions provided by the institution.

❝ If you get your school grades and meet the admissions criteria, they put you through to the entrance exam, which includes an English exam. The next step is a group aptitude test and then an interview. This definitely ensures that all the students are serious about studying at this university. **❞**

Fiona Higgins, HAAGA-HELIA, University of Applied Sciences, Finland

Costs

Higher education in Finland is free to EU students at all levels of higher education. There is no entitlement to grants or loans.

Finland is slightly more expensive than the UK, coming 10th (to the UK's 13th) in the cost of living rankings for 2011 (www.numbeo.com). It comes in lower than Norway, Denmark, Ireland and Australia. The average monthly living costs are between €700 and €900 (£603 and £775); expect to pay more in Helsinki than in smaller towns and cities. Student housing is reasonably priced; your university will support you in finding accommodation. As an EU citizen, you have the right to work in Finland, although language issues and a fairly heavy workload at university mean that this is unlikely.

> **❝** The housing is very cheap (cheaper than the UK) and relatively decent. The only thing that costs a lot is the food and the alcohol, but as long as you are aware of money, then it should work out! **❞**
>
> *Fiona Higgins, HAAGA-HELIA, University of Applied Sciences, Finland*

Most scholarships are for doctoral study or research, although institutions may have limited scholarships for students on other levels of study. Speak to your institution about this possibility. For more details, see the 'Scholarships' section at Study in Finland, www.studyinfinland.fi/tuition_and_scholarships/other_possibilities.

Sample courses
BA Plastics Technology
Arcada University of Applied Life, Helsinki
Four years
Apply from 3 January to 15 February
Tuition fees €0
Monthly living costs €600–€800 (£517–£689)

Master's degree in Physical Sciences (Astronomy)
University of Turku, Turku
Apply from 1 December to 31 January
Tuition fees €0
Monthly living costs €500–€700 (£431–£603)

PhD in Information Systems

University of Jyväskylä, Comas Graduate School, Jyväskylä

Apply by 31 March for autumn start, 30 September for spring start

Tuition fees €0

Monthly living costs €500 (£431)

> If you're interested in the Nordic countries, perhaps you would be interested in studying in Iceland. To find out more, go to Study in Iceland at www.studyiniceland.is and the ENIC-NARIC country page for Iceland at www.enic-naric. net/index.aspx?c=Iceland.

www.studyinfinland.fi

France

France is the UK's closest continental neighbour, offering good-quality education with a strong international reputation. It attracts large numbers of international students, but has very limited **English-medium** options at undergraduate level in its public universities.

> France has eight universities in the Times Higher Education World University Rankings Top 400 Universities 2011–2012.

Higher education in France

Higher education takes place in universities, *grandes écoles* and institutes of technology. The *grandes écoles* are the most prestigious and selective. They charge higher fees and require a competitive exam for entry which students may spend two years working towards (after achieving A level-standard qualifications). There may be some opportunities for the best international students at these institutions, perhaps after initial study at another university. You are advised to contact them to discuss their requirements, but you are likely to need proficiency in the French language.

France invests heavily in education; it accounts for 20% of government spending. One result of this is the low price for degrees from public universities, which are generally under €500 (£431) per year for most undergraduate and postgraduate study. Fees at public universities are set by law, while private institutions are more expensive, ranging from €3,000 to €10,000 (£2,586–£8,620) or more per year.

The fees listed below are those set for 2011/2012.

- Bachelors' degree or *licence*: three years, annual tuition fee of €177 (£152).
- Master's degree: two years, annual tuition fee of €245 (£211).
- Doctoral degree or *doctorat*: three years, annual tuition fee of €372 (£320).

> It will take at least four years to achieve a *maîtrise*, which is more like an honours degree.

The academic year starts in September or October and ends in May or June, much like the UK.

Applying

You should apply direct through the international office of your chosen institution. You can normally apply from around November. Application deadline dates vary between spring and summer, but you should apply as early as you are able.

Some institutions have a rolling programme of application and recruitment, which goes on throughout the year.

In addition to your application form and application fee, you may need to include some of the following documents:

- academic transcript
- certificates
- personal statement, to include motivation for studying and future career goals
- **letters of recommendation** (normally two)
- **research proposal** (for postgraduate research)
- copy of passport.

> The master's degree you choose depends on your future plans; choose a professional master's degree as a route to employment and a research master's degree as a route to a doctorate.

Costs

France is a reasonably expensive place to live, ranked number eight of 83 countries in the cost of living index (www.numbeo. com); that makes it more expensive than the UK, but cheaper than Norway and Australia. Campus France estimates the average monthly student budget to be €1,000 (£862) in Paris and €800 (£689) elsewhere. CNOUS, the National Centre for University and Student Welfare, holds useful information on student costs, and student life in general at www.cnous.fr.

Grants may be available to some international students through the French Ministry of Foreign and European Affairs. Entente Cordiale scholarships are awarded for postgraduate-level study. Information on these and other scholarships can be found at CampusBourses (www.campusfrance.org/fria/bourse), while

CNOUS (www.cnous.fr) has more information on the system of grants and loans. Note that application deadlines for funding may fall earlier than course application deadlines.

> If you are looking for work, the nearest CROUS centre will offer a temporary student employment service, although any vacancies are in high demand. Search on the CNOUS site for your regional CROUS office (www.cnous.fr/_vie_59.htm).

Sample courses

Bachelor of Business Administration

Ecole Supérieure de Gestion (Paris School of Business), Paris (private)

Spend one semester in USA, Europe, Australia, India, China, Israel or Mexico

Apply by July

Three years

Annual tuition fees €7,500 (£6,465)

Monthly living costs €1,000 (£862)

Master in Theoretical Physics and Applications

Cergy-Pontoise University, Cergy-Pontoise

Apply by 31 May (earlier if applying for a scholarship)

Two years

Annual tuition fees €200 (£172)

There will be additional costs for accommodation reservation services and for French language courses

Monthly living costs €600 (£517)

www.campusfrance.org/en

Germany

Germany offers a world-class education with reasonably low tuition fees in a country with the largest economy in Europe.

Higher education in Germany

In Germany, higher education is run by each of the 16 states, rather than by one central Ministry of Education. You can choose between universities, universities of applied sciences and specialist colleges of art, film or music. Universities offer the more academic options up to doctoral level, with universities of applied sciences taking a more practical approach, but only to master's level. Colleges of art, film and music offer creative or design-based courses and often have additional entry requirements to determine artistic skill or musical aptitude.

What is *numerus clausus?* This phrase relates to courses that have far more applications than there are places (medicine, dentistry, veterinary medicine and pharmacology, for example); some courses have a nationwide *numerus clausus*, while other courses may be restricted only at a particular university. If your chosen course is classed as *numerus clausus*, pay careful attention to any additional entry requirements and check how they will decide who will gain a place.

Most institutions are publicly funded, with a smaller number financed by the Church or privately funded. Most German students study at the public institutions; they are cheaper and the standard of education is comparable. At Hochskul Kompass (www.hochschulkompass.de) you can search for institutions by the way they are funded or the category of institution.

The academic year officially begins in September, although classes don't start until October. *Wintersemester* teaching runs until mid-February, while *Sommersemester* commences in April and ends in late July.

If you want to study in Germany, you'll need a
Hochschulzugangsberechtigung or university entrance
qualification. You can check whether your qualifications
are comparable at the German Academic Exchange
Service (DAAD) online admission database www.daad.de/
deutschland/wege-durchs-studium/zulassung/06550.en.html

Applying

Application processes vary between different universities and
even between different courses at the same institution. Some will
opt for a central application service, like those listed below, while
others require direct application. The best advice is to check with
the international office at your university.

Over 100 universities are members of uni-assist (www.uni-
assist.de/index_en.html), the university application service for
international students, most often used when applicants have
qualifications from outside Germany.

Applications for competitive options like medicine, dentistry,
veterinary medicine and pharmacy tend to be made through
the Foundation for Higher Education Admission at www.
hochschulstart.de. You may need to translate this website
through a service like Google Translate (translate.google.co.uk)
as it doesn't appear to be available in English. The deadline date
is 31 January.

Regardless of the system you use, you may be charged a fee for
processing and you may need to provide additional information
or evidence, including:

- certificates of qualifications achieved (your university
  will tell you how to get an authenticated copy)

- CV
- essay
- academic reference
- educational transcript
- SAT or **ACT (American College Test)** scores (see College Board for further details, http://sat.collegeboard.org/register/sat-dates)
- research proposal.

Most application processes are open between October and June or July (for an autumn start), although you should check individual deadline dates and apply in good time.

Costs

Four of the 16 states in Germany charge undergraduate tuition fees of €500 (£431) per semester (or €1,000 or £862 per year):

- Bavaria
- Baden-Württemberg
- Hamburg
- Lower Saxony.

The remaining 12 states do not charge tuition fees.

In addition to any fees, higher education institutions across the country charge semester contributions; this covers certain administration charges and should entitle you to student discounts and free public transport. The cost varies between institutions; you should budget for around €200 (£172) per semester.

Fees at postgraduate level range from €650 (£560) to a few thousand euros per semester. It is important to note that fees at private universities and colleges will be considerably higher, in some cases as much as €20,000 (£17,241) per year.

Students in Germany live on an average of €770 (£663) per month, according to information provided by DAAD. Germany is ranked number 21 of 83 countries on a 2011 cost of living ranking (www.numbeo.com), so living there should be cheaper than the UK, but also cheaper than New Zealand, Cyprus, Canada and Singapore.

Any scholarships are unlikely to cover all costs. Scholarships are limited; this is particularly the case for undergraduate study. Search on the DAAD Scholarship Database and ask your university about their opportunities, www.daad.de/deutschland/ foerderung/stipendiendatenbank/00462.en.html.

Sample courses

BSc Applied Biology
Bonn-Rhein-Sieg University of Applied Sciences, Sankt Augustin
Three years
Restricted admission, so preference goes to applicants with the highest grades
Direct application by 15 July
Tuition fees €0
Monthly living costs €600 (£517)

MA Contemporary East Asian Studies
University of Duisberg-Essen (Institute of East Asian Studies), Essen
Two years
Direct application by 15 September
Tuition fees €1,000 (£862)
Monthly living costs €600 (£517)

Alternatives to Germany might include Austria, Liechtenstein or Switzerland. Discover education in Austria at OeAD (Austrian Agency for International Mobility), www.oead.at/welcome_to_austria/education_research/EN. You can research opportunities in Liechtenstein through ENIC-NARIC, www.enic-naric.net/index.aspx?c=Liechtenstein. Find out more about higher education in Switzerland at the Rectors' Conference of the Swiss Universities at www.crus.ch/information-programme/study-in-switzerland.html?L=2.

www.study-in.de/en

Ireland

Ireland is close to home and English-speaking, with a higher education system that has much in common with the UK system. It is therefore a popular choice among UK students.

Higher education in Ireland

Degrees can be awarded by universities and by a number of institutes of technology. Other higher education institutions exist, where qualifications are awarded through HETAC, the Higher Education and Training Awards Council (www.hetac.ie). A number of the higher education institutions in Ireland are private. For a list, see the Education in Ireland website, www.educationireland.ie/index.php?option=com_content&view=article&id=27&Itemid=36.

For general information on education in Ireland, go to the Irish Council for International Students website, www.icosirl.ie.

Trinity College Dublin tops the two Irish universities on
the Times Higher Education World University Rankings
Top 400 2011/2012. It is ranked number 117 (just above
the universities of York and Southampton). University
College Dublin also features at number 159 (just below the
University of Warwick).

The qualifications on offer differ slightly from England, Scotland
and Northern Ireland in that a three year ordinary degree
is available, as well as a three- or four-year honours degree
(Scotland offers a similar choice). The grading system (first,
upper second, lower second and so on) echoes the UK. Taught
and research master's degrees should take one to two years, with
doctorates taking a minimum of three years' research.

You can search for undergraduate and postgraduate courses
through the Qualifax Course Finder (www.qualifax.ie).
Postgraduate options can be found through Postgrad Ireland
(http://postgradireland.com).

Applying

While the academic year is in line with the UK, running from
September to June, the application system has its differences.
Undergraduate applications are based on actual grades (and an
admissions test, in some cases) and little else, so offers aren't
made until results come out.

Entry requirements

The A level requirements for most degrees can make Irish
universities a challenge to enter. They tend to be looking for
academic subjects that echo those taken at school in Ireland. If
you are applying with different qualifications, you should speak
to the university international office or admissions office in

advance; they may need to evaluate your qualifications before you apply.

Most degree-level programmes ask for three Cs at A level, or equivalent, as a minimum requirement. For the more competitive courses, like medicine, they ask for particularly high grades. In the scoring system for A levels, grade A* at A level is worth 150 points and grade E is worth 40. (For full details, see the Central Applications Office website at www.cao.ie/index. php?page=scoring&s=gce.)

At universities and associated colleges, your best four A levels (or three, plus an AS in a different subject) will be considered up to a maximum of 600 points. Some institutions will consider different combinations of A level and AS level grades, so may be accessible for those without four A levels.

Entry to medicine

For 2012 entry to medicine, applicants must have at least 480 points (which can be obtained from four Bs at A level, for example), plus any minimum requirements from their university. Both exam results and HPAT scores will be considered when offering a place. See Undergraduate Entry to Medicine brochure for more details (www2.cao.ie/downloads/ documents/2012UGMedEntry.pdf).

The Health Professions Admission Test (HPAT, www.hpat-ireland.acer.edu.au) is required for undergraduate entry to medicine, while the Graduate Medical School Admissions Test (GAMSAT, http://gamsat.acer.edu.au/gamsat-ireland) is needed for applications to postgraduate medicine. Application dates are often early and examination dates may be restricted to a single day.

Applying

You can apply online or on paper through the Central Applications Office (CAO) at www.cao.ie. Applications should be made by 1 February or earlier, particularly for restricted entry courses, although there is a late closing date for other courses of 1 May. In most cases, there is no need for references or a personal statement. A fee is charged for processing.

Postgraduate applications

Postgraduate applications can be made direct to your chosen university, often via the international office. Some institutions use the Postgraduate Applications Centre (PAC) at www.pac. ie. Closing dates vary, even within a single institution. In most cases, a minimum of a 2:2 grade in an undergraduate honours degree is required for a master's degree.

In addition to the application form and fee, you may need to include an academic transcript, references, a CV, a research proposal (where relevant) and a statement of interest, explaining your motivation, commitment and what you hope to achieve.

Postgraduate research at Trinity College Dublin can be applied for at any time. Each programme of taught postgraduate study has an individual deadline; many programmes require applications by 30 June, but you should check for your chosen course.

Costs

UK students on their first full-time undergraduate degree should not have to pay tuition fees. However, you will be required to pay a student contribution or registration fee of a maximum €2,000 (£1,724) in 2011/2012.

According to Postgrad Ireland, you can expect postgraduate fees of over €4,000 (£3,448) for research degrees, with taught programmes ranging from under €4,000 (£3,448) to as much as €29,500 (£25,431) for an MBA.

At number six (out of 83 countries) on a 2011 cost of living ranking, Ireland is a little more expensive than the UK (see www. numbeo.com for more detail). In the Republic of Ireland, Dublin is the most expensive place to live. Education in Ireland estimates that, on average, a student can expect to spend between €7,500 and €12,000 (£6,465 and £13,344) per year; of course, this will depend on where you live and the lifestyle you choose.

Sample courses
BA (Hons) Anthropology
National University of Ireland, Maynooth
Three years
Apply through CAO by 1 February
€2,000 (£1,724) registration fee
Living costs not provided

MSc European Employment Studies (taught)
Trinity College Dublin
One year
Direct application by 30 June
Annual fees €8,750 (£7,543)
Estimated living costs €10,400 (£8,965) for one academic year

www.educationireland.ie

Italy

Higher education in Italy
The majority of universities in Italy are state-funded, although there is a range of alternative provision including non-state

universities, universities for foreigners (focussing on Italian language, literature and culture), specialist postgraduate schools and telematic (or distance learning) universities. Most programmes are taught in Italian; English-medium opportunities in Italy are most often found at private universities and colleges. Although the options for a full degree may be limited, Italy remains a popular destination for students on Erasmus exchanges.

The academic year runs from September or October until July. The qualifications on offer are a three-year *laurea* which is the Italian bachelor's degree, the two-year *laurea specialista* which is comparable to a master's degree, while the *dottore magistrale* is comparable to a doctorate. Much of the assessment in Italian higher education is exam-based.

> ❝ The cost of study is quite similar to the UK, here one can also apply for scholarships and one can get reduced fees, if needed. It is less expensive than the US schools. ❞
>
> *Sema Ali, University of Bocconi, Italy*

Applying

Provided you meet the general entry requirements for higher education in the UK and have completed 12 years of education, you can be considered for undergraduate study in Italy. If you have a bachelor's degree, you can be considered for a master's degree and if you have a master's degree, you can consider applying for a doctorate. You should apply direct to individual institutions, who may set their own additional entry requirements. Application forms can be found on the Study in Italy website, www.study-in-italy.it, although you should discuss the process and timescale with your university's international office before you apply.

Costs

Fees are set by the individual institutions. You should expect to pay up to €1,000 (£862) per year in the public institutions and more with the private providers, although these might still end up costing less than many of the courses in the UK. For living costs, Italy is fairly similar to the UK. It is ranked 11th (to the UK's 13th) in the cost of living rankings for 2011 at www.numbeo.com.

> **66** University of Bocconi is very international, with students from all over the world. The classes are taught in English and it is a very broad based business curriculum. The professors are very knowledgeable and the classes are not very big, unlike schools I considered in the States, where some undergraduate classes had hundreds of students in them. The professors are also very friendly and accessible. **99**
>
> *Sema Ali, University of Bocconi, Italy*

Sample courses

Laurea (bachelor's) degree in Applied Computer Science (online learning)
University of Urbino
Three years
Apply from July to October
Tuition fees €1,731 (£1,492)
Living costs not applicable

Master's degree in Economics and Political Science
University of Milan, Milan

Two years

Apply between March and September

Tuition fees €0 (although entry will be competitive)

Monthly living costs of up to €1,000 (£862)

> If you want an alternative to Italy, you might have
> wondered about Greece, although few international students
> choose Greece for their studies. You can find out more at the
> Greek Ministry of Education (www.minedu.gov.gr).

www.study-in-italy.it

Netherlands

Interest in the Netherlands as a study venue has been growing
steadily, with the Dutch universities keen to attract international
students and offering hundreds of programmes taught entirely
in English.

> The Netherlands has an impressive 12 universities in
> the Times Higher Education World University Rankings
> 2011/2012 Top 200.

Higher education in the Netherlands

The style of teaching in the Netherlands is interactive and
student-centred, with a focus on problem-based learning. The
academic year runs from early September to late June.

You can opt to study at a research-based university (WO) or
a University of Applied Sciences (HBO), which offers more
vocational options. An academic or research-orientated bachelor's
degree (WO) takes three years, while the applied alternative
(HBO) would take four years, with the chance of a work

placement and often a **study abroad** opportunity. Associate degrees take two years, with the option to move on to an applied bachelor's degree.

> **❝** The standard of teaching is very high – the professors and lecturers are interesting speakers and knowledgeable on their subject but, like any university, putting in the work is down to the student. **❞**
>
> *Clare Higgins, The Hague University of Applied Sciences (De Haagse Hogeschool), the Netherlands*

> **❝** I decided on Amsterdam because of the university, not the other way around. Small class sizes, a real focus on diversity and an open (liberal arts) degree definitely played a big role in my initial attraction to the institution. **❞**
>
> *Shanna Hanbury, Amsterdam University College, the Netherlands*

At master's level, you again have the choice between a research-based degree (WO) or the applied route (HBO), both of which take one to two years. In contrast, doctorates are only available through the research universities (WO).

To find a course, you can browse the NUFFIC database at http://ispacsearch.nuffic.nl/ or use Study in Holland's database at http://studyinholland.co.uk/what_to_study.html.

Applying

In most cases, two or three A levels, or equivalent, should be sufficient to meet the requirements for most bachelor's degrees. If you studied an alternative qualification, you should discuss it with your chosen university. At postgraduate level, you will

need a bachelor's degree to progress to a master's. It is likely
that any offer you receive will require you to pass your courses,
rather than achieve specific grades. Although getting a place at
university may seem easier than in the UK, the university will
need you to prove your capability in the first year. Students who
can't cope academically will be asked to leave the course.

In some popular subjects like medicine or law, places may be
restricted through a scheme known as *numerus fixus*. For
these courses, the allocation of places is decided through
a slightly complicated lottery system, which can vary
according to the requirements of the university; talk to
your chosen institution to gain an understanding of how to
give yourself the best chance of success.

Studielink

You can apply to public institutions at undergraduate and
postgraduate level through Studielink (http://info.studielink.nl/
en/studenten/Pages/Default.aspx) from October onwards. You can
choose up to four options, including one *numerus fixus* course.
Requirements for supporting documentation vary, but could
include:

- certificates
- **academic transcript**
- personal statement or **letter of motivation** indicating
  why you are applying
- copy of passport
- CV
- two **letters of recommendation**
- **research proposal** (where relevant).

For some postgraduate study, an admissions test like GRE (www.
ets.org/gre) or GMAT (www.mba.com) will be needed. In all cases,

your institution will be able to tell you whether they require application through Studielink and any supporting information they need.

Most courses have an application deadline of 1 June, although *numerus fixus* courses require an earlier application. You can find a helpful guide to Studielink at the Study in Holland website, www.studyinholland.co.uk/studielink.html. Some courses will require a direct application instead.

The application process at university colleges differs, in that it requires an earlier application that should be made direct; another key difference is that students are invited to interview.

> **❝** I had to write a personal statement and an essay. I was out of Europe when I applied so they did the interview over Skype. They were also fine with me scanning and emailing a lot of the documents, which was a huge help. **❞**
>
> *Shanna Hanbury, Amsterdam University College,*
> *the Netherlands*

Costs

In the public universities, you can expect annual fees starting at around €1,700 (£1,465) at undergraduate level and something similar at postgraduate level. This can be paid upfront or through an instalment system.

Undergraduate students aged under 30 who work for at least 32 hours per month should be entitled to a basic grant of around €260 (£224) per month (2011/2012), with the possibility of topping this up further with a supplementary means-tested grant. Access to grants at postgraduate level varies. EU undergraduate and postgraduate students can take out a student loan for tuition fees from the Netherlands. You can find out more about loans and grants at DUO-IB-Groep (Department of Education), www.ib-groep.nl/International_visitors/EU_EEA_students/Grant_for_tuition_or_course_fees.asp.

Scholarships are also available. You can search for a scholarship through NUFFIC's Grantfinder at www.nuffic.nl/international-students/scholarships/grantfinder.

At number seven out of 83 countries on the 2011 Numbeo (www.numbeo.com) cost of living ranking, the Netherlands is not cheap; it is comparable in living expenses to Ireland or France.

> **❝** I pay €289.81 (£249) a month for a shared space in student accommodation, with bills included. It's not a lot of space, but it's reasonable and nice. You don't spend any money on transportation because you bike everywhere.
>
> Food is very expensive here, definitely more than in the UK. I usually spend about €20 (£17.24) at the supermarket for a well-rounded shopping list, but if I go to the Turkish shops it's cheaper, around €10 (£8.62). **❞**
>
> *Shanna Hanbury, Amsterdam University College,*
> *the Netherlands*

Sample courses
BSc Psychology
University of Groningen, Groningen
Three years
Apply by 15 May through Studielink *(numerus fixus)*
Annual tuition fees €1,771 (£1,526)
Annual living costs €9,000–€9,500 (£7,758–£8,189)

MA in Photography
Avans University of Applied Sciences, Breda
Two years
Apply directly by 25 June
Annual tuition fees €1,713 (£1,476)
Monthly living costs €700–€1,000 (£603–£862)

www.nuffic.nl/international-students

Norway

With around 14,000 students from overseas and no fees at public
universities, how about studying in Norway? It offers many
postgraduate courses in English, although only a handful at
bachelor's degree level. Norway has high costs but one of the best
standards of living in the world; it has been ranked top by the
UN for the past four years. It can be cold, but you will discover a
great outdoor lifestyle.

> 66 Within the first month of arriving here, I'd been
> on fishing trips, hiking trips, whizzing around in
> a little rib boat on the Saltstraumen, swimming in some of
> the most beautiful lakes which are a 15 minute walk from
> the university, and even met the Norwegian Prime Minister.
> It's been quite something! 99
> *Megan Doxford, University of Nordland, Norway*

Higher education in Norway

Higher education takes place at universities, specialised
university institutions, university colleges or national colleges
of the arts. Universities have a research focus, while university
colleges focus on professional studies. It is possible to gain a
master's degree and sometimes even a doctorate at a university

college. Most higher education institutions in Norway are state-funded, although there are some private university colleges. In Norway, you would generally study a three-year bachelor's degree, a two-year master's and a three-year doctorate. The academic year runs from mid-August to mid-June.

> It is common for students in Norway to take time out to work or travel before university, so they may be a little older.

You can search for study opportunities through Study in Norway at www.studyinnorway.no.

Applying

According to the GSU list (the list of minimum requirements for admission to Norwegian higher education), you will need five subjects in total, including two A levels (or one A level and two AS levels); you could make up the other two or three subjects from GCSEs. Students from Scotland will need to pass five Highers. Some subjects will have additional requirements. You can find the GSU list at the Norwegian Agency for Quality Assurance in HE (NOKUT) website www.nokut.no. Successful completion of a bachelor's degree is needed to progress to master's level.

You should apply direct to your chosen institution sometime between December and March for courses starting in August. Application deadlines vary, but your institution will be able to advise on specific deadline dates, as well as any supplementary information needed. This could include:

- academic transcript
- copies of certificates, for qualifications already gained
- CV
- research proposal, where necessary.

> 66 The application process was very simple and relatively hassle-free. Everything was done online and they only required a few documents such as my undergraduate transcripts, my CV and some essays I was required to write to apply for a scholarship. A GMAT score was also required. 99
>
> *John Magee, BI Norwegian Business School, Norway*

Costs

Whether you are studying at undergraduate level or for a master's degree or a PhD, you are unlikely to have to pay fees at a state-funded university or university college. There is a small semester fee of NOK300–600 (£33–£66), which gives you a student discount card along with membership of student welfare associations, access to campus health services, sports facilities and so on. Private institutions charge fees, although these should still be lower than those charged by universities in the UK, perhaps with the exception of some MBAs.

There are some scholarships available for study in Norway. See the Study in Norway website for details.

Living costs in Norway are high; in fact, it ranks number one out of 83 countries in a 2011 cost of living index, see www.numbeo. com. You should expect to have at the very least NOK8,900 (£980) per month for living expenses.

See the case study on page 255 for tips on managing on a budget in Norway.

> ❝ The price of living is very high, so the Norwegian Government requests you have ample funds for the year ahead. You have to have 90,000NOK (£9,900) in a Norwegian bank account in order to be accepted. This is the amount of money needed to survive a year at university out here. It is possible to get work, which helps an awful lot financially, especially as the minimum wage is a lot higher than in the UK. ❞
>
> *Megan Doxford, University of Nordland, Norway*

Sample courses

BA in Circumpolar Studies
University of Nordland, Bodø
Three years
Apply direct by April 1
Tuition fees NOK0
Living expenses NOK40,000 (£4,400) per semester

MSc Marine Biology
University of Bergen
Two years
Apply directly by 1 December, 2:1 required
Tuition fees NOK0
Living expenses NOK9,080 (£998) per month

www.studyinnorway.no

Spain

Although the option to study in Spain on an exchange programme is a popular one for UK students, opportunities for a full degree are limited; most options at public institutions are taught in Spanish. This looks set to change as the Spanish government is keen to recruit more international students. There are already opportunities in private institutions, which make up around a third of the higher education institutions in Spain.

Higher education in Spain

> 66 Education here is inspiring; young vibrant professors who are passionate about what they do and who also seem to be inspired by their own students too. 99
>
> *Esme Alexander, IE University, Spain*
>
> 66 My university offers smaller classes, far more interesting lectures, one to one help if needed and access to far better facilities (apart from sporting). 99
>
> *Eleanor Spooner, IE University, Spain*

Universidad.es is developing a searchable database of courses. You can also find information through the Ministry of Education at www.educacion.es.

Undergraduate degrees take from three years, master's degrees last one or two years while doctorates take from two years. Some of the private universities offer accelerated programmes to reduce the length of study.

Applying

As long as you have the general qualifications to access HE in the UK, you should meet the general requirements for HE in Spain. Talk direct to your chosen university about their application procedures. You may need to apply through UNED at www.uned.es for evaluation of your qualifications. (Note: you may need to translate this page using a service like Google Translate.)

Completion of a bachelor's degree in the UK or the European Higher Education Area will satisfy the general requirements of a master's degree. Sixty ECTS credits are required to progress to research at doctoral level.

> **❝** The university application process explored your whole range of interest and motivations. It was personal and comprehensive, wanting to derive the best aspects from their applicants. **❞**
>
> *Esme Alexander, IE University, Spain*

Costs

A bachelor's degree or *grado* at a public university will cost €535 to €1,280 (£461 to £1,103) per year (2011/2012). At private universities, fees start at €5,335 (£4,599), but can be considerably higher than this, although these institutions often have generous schemes of financial support. Master's *(máster)* and doctoral *(doctorado)* degrees are paid for per credit; a master's course comprising 60 ECTS credits may cost between €995 and €1,920 (£857 and £1,655). Private institutions set their own fees, but these must still fall within government limits.

Scholarships are available and can be searched through the Universidad website at www.universidad.es/information_and_resources/scholarships. You can also ask the international office of your chosen university.

Living costs are lower than in a number of the European countries mentioned in this chapter. Spain is ranked number 30 out of 83 countries in a cost of living survey for 2011 (see www.numbeo.com), comparing favourably to the UK at number 13. Prices in the major cities can be much higher.

Sample courses

Bachelor's degree in International Business Economics
Pompeu Fabra University, Barcelona (public institution)
Four years
Apply direct to the university
Annual tuition fees €1,047 (£902)
Monthly living costs €800 (£689)

MSc International Relations
IE Business School, Madrid (private institution)
10 months
Direct applications accepted throughout the year
Annual tuition fees €30,200 (£26,034) although a range of
financial aid packages are available
Monthly living costs €1260–€1860*(£1,086–£1603)

MBA Global Banking and Finance
European University, Barcelona (private university)
12 months
Apply throughout the year, admissions on a rolling basis
Annual tuition fee €14,400 (£12,413)
Monthly living costs from €1,450* (£1,250)

*The figures for living costs provided by the private universities
appear to be much higher than estimates given by public
institutions.

Interested in studying in Portugal? Nearly all courses are
in Portuguese, but you can find out more at DGES (General
Directorate for Higher Education) at www.dges.mctes.pt/
DGES/pt.

www.universidad.es/home_en/lang.en

Sweden

30,000 international students currently choose Sweden for
their studies. With a strong focus on innovation and a forward-
thinking, student-centred academic environment, Swedish higher
education has much to offer.

> Five Swedish institutions are in the Times Higher Education
> World University Rankings Top 200 2011/2012.

Higher education in Sweden

The academic year runs from late August to early June and
is divided into two semesters. Three-year bachelor's degrees
or *kandidatexamen* are the norm. A master's degree or
masterexamen will take one to two years, while doctoral research
or *doktorsexamen* takes at least four years.

Higher education takes place in universities and university
colleges, with universities the only institutions with the
automatic right to issue doctoral degrees. Local collaboration
is widespread, so many institutions offer options reflecting the
needs of local industries and businesses.

> The name of the institution will not always reveal whether
> it is a university or university college; most university
> colleges will call themselves universities, while some
> universities are called *högskola* (or university college) in
> Swedish. Degrees awarded by both types of institution are
> equivalent to one another.

You can search for study options at Study in Sweden, www.
studyinsweden.se/Course-search.

Applying

Any qualification that gives you access to higher education in the UK should do the same for undergraduate studies in Sweden. Individual institutions then set their own procedures for selecting applicants; this might include grades, assessment of samples of work, interviews, admissions tests or work experience. Your institution's international office will be able to advise further about any special requirements.

For bachelor's and master's degrees, applications are made online through University Admissions at www.universityadmissions. se. Deadlines are generally around mid-January for August start and mid-August for any courses starting in spring. At doctoral level, applications are made direct to the institution and often to the specific department, accompanied by copies of certificates, academic transcripts and letters of recommendation. Check any deadline dates with your academic department.

Costs

In most cases, university courses in Sweden are tuition free, although student union membership fees are payable at SEK50–350 (£4.65–£32.58) per semester. A range of scholarships are available at Study in Sweden (www.studyinsweden.se/ Scholarships). Ask your institution about any scholarships that they administer.

An average monthly budget for a student is around SEK7,070. Sweden is ranked number nine out of 83 countries in Numbeo's 2011 cost of living table at www.numbeo.com, which makes it cheaper than the Netherlands and France.

Sample courses

Bachelor's degree in Peace and Conflict Studies
Malmö University, Malmö
Three years

experience.algomau.ca

SMALL UNIVERSITY
BIG EDUCATION

A Community of Students Learning Together.

Algoma University is committed to placing you first. Our professors encourage interaction, discussion & independent thought in small classroom settings. At Algoma University you get the support, guidance & mentoring you need to succeed. Here is your chance to make new friends from every corner of the world!

- Internationally recognized degrees
- A welcoming & diverse campus
- Competitive international fees
- Undergraduate degree & certificate programs
- Never more than 65 students in a class
- A true Canadian experience in the heart of the Great Lakes in Sault Ste. Marie, Ontario

Contact us! international@algomau.ca

university of groningen

Go Dutch - Study in Holland

400 years of passion and performance

Over 90 degree programs in English in virtually every field

www.rug.nl

Seneca

STUDY AT SENECA 🍁

Over 140 programs, including Bachelor's Degrees and Graduate Certificates in:

> Art & Design
> Business Studies
> Computer Studies
> Engineering Technology
> Science

VISIT US ONLINE:
STUDYATSENECA.CA

CONTACT:
seneca.international@senecac.on.ca

APPLY TODAY

SENECA COLLEGE | TORONTO, CANADA

THE UNIVERSITY OF THE WEST INDIES
MONA, JAMAICA

Are you a full time student?

Interested in studying abroad?

Live the dream

APPLICATION DEADLINES
March 1 for full time degree programmes and Semester 1
October 1 for Semester 11

FOR MORE DETAILED INFORMATION CONTACT:
The International Students Office, Annex Building,
Tel: (876) 702-3737 **OR** (876) 970-6890/3
Email: isomona@uwimona.edu.jm

www.mona.uwi.edu/iss/

The UWI, Mona offers a wide range of programmes including:

HUMANITIES & EDUCATION
- Cultural Studies
- Entertainment & Cultural Enterprise Management
- History & Archaeology
- Library & Information Studies
- Journalism
- Linguistics
- Modern Languages, including Chinese and Japanese

LAW
- 3-year programme at Mona

MEDICAL SCIENCES
- MBBS
- Dentistry
- Diagnostic Imaging (Radiography)
- Basic Medical Sciences
- Physical Therapy
- Nursing
- Public Health

PURE & APPLIED SCIENCES
- Applied & Food Chemistry
- Geography & Geology
- Actuarial Science
- Information Technology
- Marine Biology
- Mathematics & Modelling Processes
- Tropical Horticulture

SOCIAL SCIENCES
- Economics
- Banking & Finance
- Entrepreneurship
- Psychology
- Labour & Employment Relations
- Social Work
- Hotel & Tourism Management
- Management Studies
- WEEKEND PROGRAMMES AVAILABLE

INSTITUTE FOR GENDER AND DEVELOPMENT STUDIES
- Gender and Development

WESTERN JAMAICA CAMPUS
- Banking and Finance
- Digital Media Production
- Management Studies,
- Management Information Systems
- Psychology
- Nursing
- MBA programme (concentrations in Marketing, Banking and Finance)

STUDENT CENTRED PROGRAMMES
- Leadership training
- Mentorship programme
- Study Abroad
- Co-curricular activities
- Online Masters programmes

UWI
Inspiring Excellence, Producing Leaders

Where innovation starts

Bachelor program
**Computer Science &
Engineering**
now in English!

Interested in general computer
science and technologies?
Choose Software Science

WEB SCIENCE

Interested in new developments
relating to the web?
Choose Web Science

More information? Check **www.tue.nl/bachelorprograms/CSE**

TU/e Technische Universiteit
Eindhoven
University of Technology

INTERNATIONAL MSc PROGRAMME IN SUSTAINABLE ENERGY AT REYKJAVIK UNIVERSITY ICELAND

REYST

REYST is a graduate programme in sustainable energy, offered by Reykjavik University. It endeavors to promote the advancement of sustainable energy use by enhancing understanding of the science underlying energy resources, the technology to improve their utilization and the business knowledge of bringing good solutions to market.

The REYST programme admits students once a year and starts at the beginning of August. Application deadlines are as follows:

- **Students outside EEA: February 1.**
- **Students from EEA countries: April 4.**

For further information please contact
Kristin Kristinsdottir, program administrator:

Email: reyst@ru.is
Telephone: +354 599 6557
www.reyst.is

STUDY BUSINESS OR MARKETING IN THE HEART OF THE NETHERLANDS!

WWW.INTERNATIONAL.HU.NL

HU

UNIVERSITY OF APPLIED SCIENCES UTRECHT

High Quality, Low Fees

At University College Roosevelt Academy you can

- Study at one of the top-ten English-speaking universities in Europe
- Create your own program by choosing your own combination of subjects
- Follow our alumni to Oxford, Cambridge or into any other European or American research institute

For an annual tuition fee of just £1500!

Roosevelt Academy

Universiteit Utrecht

www.roac.nl

HZ UNIVERSITY OF APPLIED SCIENCES

Vlissingen

Bachelor degrees:
Chemistry | Civil Engineering | Delta Management | International Business & Management Studies
Water Management | International Maintenance Management | Vitality & Tourism Management

THE NETHERLANDS | WWW.HZ.NL **WHERE STUDENTS MATTER**

THE NEXT STEP IN HOSPITALITY

Hotel Management School Maastricht ZU YD

· Become a manager or entrepreneur in the hospitality industry
· One of the leading hotel management schools in the world
· Inspiring programme where innovation comes first
· International internships take you all over the world
· Real life training in our Teaching Hotel
· Excellent facilities; rooms available on campus

www.hotelschoolmaastricht.nl

Amsterdam University College
AUC

Excellence and Diversity in a Global City

→ A residential honours college of the University of Amsterdam and VU University Amsterdam.

→ Offers an international liberal arts and sciences bachelor honours programme that crosses the boundaries of languages, cultures and academic disciplines.

→ Attracts students from all over the world, who engage in intensive and small-scale seminars with high calibre international staff on a daily basis.

→ Discussions start from 'Big Questions' in science and society and lead to in-depth study in a wide range of disciplines.

→ Substantial focus is placed on the sciences, including interdisciplinary themes such as: Health and Well-being; Energy, Climate and Sustainability; and Life, Evolution, and the Universe.

www.AUC.nl

UNIVERSITY OF AMSTERDAM

 VU UNIVERSITY AMSTERDAM

Hogeschool van Arnhem en Nijmegen
HAN University of Applied Sciences

HAN UNIVERSITY OF APPLIED SCIENCES

Bachelor Courses in English
- Automotive Engineering
- Business Management Studies (HRQM)
- Communication
- International Business and Management Studies
- Finance and Control
- Logistics Management (Economics)
- Life Sciences

Study in the Netherlands
HAN University of Applied Sciences offers you international diversity, small classes of 30 students, high-tech facilities, a personal approach, internships at international companies and an accredited Bachelor diploma.

THE WORLD IS YOURS...
GO INTERNATIONAL!

HAN www.han.nl/english

Windesheim university
OF APPLIED SCIENCES

START IN
SEPTEMBER
OR FEBRUARY

Visit our website: www.windesheimhonourscollege.nl

ENGLISH TAUGHT BBA IN HOLLAND

Managing for a sustainable world

Rotterdam
Business School

Gain practical experience and build your international network, while acquiring the knowledge and skills you need for a successful career in international business.

Our English taught programmes include:
→ International Business and Management Studies (BBA)
→ International Business and Languages (BBA)
→ Trade Management for Asia (BBA)
→ Master in Finance and Accounting
→ Master in Consultancy and Entrepreneurship
→ Master in Logistics Management
→ Executive MBA (part-time)
→ Preparation course - Bachelor
→ Preparation course - Master
→ Summer School

rotterdambusinessschool.nl

For more information about our programmes and practical information about tuition fees and housing please contact our Global Recruitment and Student Support team (GR&SS):
Ⓣ +31 (0)10 794 62 50
Ⓔ rbs@hr.nl

exceed
expectations

ROTTERDAM UNIVERSITY

UNIVERSITY OF APPLIED SCIENCES

Universiteit Utrecht

Study at the best university in the Netherlands?

www.uu.nl/internationalstudents

WAGENINGEN UNIVERSITY

Food | Earth & Environment | Technology | Economics & Social Sciences | Health | Nature & Agriculture

- Voted best university in the Netherlands for the seventh year in a row

- In top 100 of the Times Higher Education World University Rankings

- Located in the centre of the Netherlands

- 28 Master of Science programmes

- 2 year programmes taught in English

WAGENINGEN UNIVERSITY
WAGENINGEN UR

WWW.WAGENINGENUNIVERSITY.EU

PARENTS! With 83 applicants for every graduate job how can your child beat the competition?

Help your child:
- ✓ Land key internships
- ✓ Find jobs to apply for
- ✓ Excel at the interview

For more information visit www.trotman.co.uk

a parent's guide to

GRADUATE JOBS

How to help your child get a job after uni

Paul Radmond

trotman t

THE **HAGUE**
UNIVERSITY OF
APPLIED SCIENCES

SUPPOSE YOU...

... study in the international
city of **peace and justice**

International Bachelor Studies

- European Studies
- Industrial Design Engineering
- International Business and Management Studies
- International Communication Management
- International Financial Management and Control
- Law
- Process and Food Technology
- Public Management
- Safety and Security Management Studies

International Master Studies

- Master in Accounting and Control
- Master of Business Administration
- Master in International Communication Management

www.thehagueuniversity.nl

H/ THE HAGUE UNIVERSITY OF APPLIED SCIENCES MAKES YOU THINK

UNIVERSITY OF AMSTERDAM

Study a Master's for a fair price in a global city close to home

Over 120 Master's programmes taught in English

The University of Amsterdam (UvA) has one of the largest selections of international Master's study programmes of any university in Europe. More than 120 programmes are taught in English, including a number of Bachelor programme options. Some of these programmes are unique and can be found only at the UvA.

Value for your money

The UvA has an excellent international reputation and offers high-quality study programmes at competitive prices. EU citizens will pay only €1,771 in tuition fees for the 2012-2013 academic year.

Prime location

Amsterdam is well connected for travel in Europe, and has excellent links to the rest of the world. As a capital city and centre of culture and commerce, Amsterdam offers students access to a wide range of arts, entertainment and social activities.

Career potential

Numerous Dutch and international firms, academic institutions and cultural organisations make Amsterdam the commercial, social and artistic heart of the Netherlands and a prestigious global centre. Students benefit from having access to major corporations both during their study and after completing their programme.

Visit our website www.uva.nl/isp for more information about our study programmes and application.

Discover the world of
Jacobs University

JACOBS
UNIVERSITY

Study in Germany

_ You're looking for a place that offers a world-class education in English?
_ You're not afraid to face academic challenges?
_ You want to make a difference in the world?
_ You will never settle for simple answers?
_ You always dreamed of exploring new cultures?
_ You want to study on a campus that calls the world home?

*We prepare the leaders of tomorrow to responsibly
meet global challenges.*

To learn more, contact us at:
admission@jacobs-university.de

Jacobs University
Campus Ring 1 | 28759 Bremen | Germany

jacobs-university.de

LOOKING FURTHER INTO VU UNIVERSITY AMSTERDAM

14 INTERDISCIPLINARY
RESEARCH INSTITUTES

12 FACULTIES

150 RESEARCH
PROGRAMMES

OVER 70
PROGRAMMES
TAUGHT IN ENGLISH

CAMPUS UNIVERSITY
IN AMSTERDAM

OVER 24.000
STUDENTS

WWW.VUAMSTERDAM.COM

OUTSTANDING
EDUCATION AND
RESEARCH

VU
UNIVERSITY
AMSTERDAM

LOOKING FURTHER

Hanze
University of Applied Sciences
Groningen

Want to study abroad? Come to Groningen, the Netherlands.

Your talent is the foundation for your success and growth. At Hanze University of Applied Sciences, Groningen, we challenge you to use this talent to its full potential. We are dedicated to providing you with every opportunity to develop and grow. We only ask that you go on to share your talent and move the world.

We offer:

- Bachelor and master programmes
- Quality and practice-oriented education
- Value for money
- Two work placements
- Access to our international professional network
- Personal attention
- The opportunity to study in Groningen, city of talent.

To learn more about Hanze University of Applied Sciences, Groningen, visit: **www.hanzegroningen.eu**

share **your talent.** move **the world.**

Apply via www.universityadmissions.se from December to 17
January
Tuition fees SEK0
Monthly living costs SEK7,300 (£679)

Master's Programme in Biomedicine
Karolinska Institutet, Stockholm
Two years
Apply via www.universityadmissions.se from October to
16 January
Tuition fees SEK0
Monthly living costs SEK7,500 (£698)

www.studyinsweden.se

Pros and cons of study in Europe

Pros

- Relatively close to home.
- Often cheaper for tuition fees than much of the UK.
- No visa restrictions.
- Able to work and to stay on after study.

Cons

- Language issues.
- Some countries have high costs of living.
- Pressure to do well in first year to remain on the
  course.

Reykjavik University: a vibrant international university

Reykjavik University (RU) is Iceland's largest private university. Based in the heart of Iceland's capital, it focuses on educating students to become entrepreneurial leaders in society.

Reykjavik University has four Schools: Law, Business, Computer Science, and Science and Engineering. Each School offers high-quality teaching, excellent research facilities and student support services. The University is committed to quality; the academic programmes are based on internationally recognised models, and are regularly reviewed and improved by the University.

Reykjavik University is an international university with strong links to the local and international academic and business communities. Our aim is to meet the needs of local and international students through a wide choice of innovative academic courses at undergraduate and graduate level, as well as through a range of Executive Education programmes for professionals.

The more than 3,000 students at Reykjavik University are supported by over 500 employees. Our faculty comes from 26 different countries, with graduates from many of the world's most respected universities. In addition to its strong academic qualification, the faculty has extensive practical experience.

Visiting faculty from world-renowned universities travel to Reykjavik to teach courses at the University. Among them are professors from IESE Business School, the Instituto de Empresa, Harvard University, Boston University, Copenhagen Business School and London Business School.

Reykjavik University offers graduate studies that are taught in English as well as a large number of undergraduate courses that are taught in English for exchange students. It is very easy for English-speaking students to get by in Iceland.

REYST: Reykjavik Energy Graduate School of Sustainable Systems

REYST, a graduate programme offered by Reykjavik University in collaboration with leading industrial partners, Reykjavik Energy and Iceland Geosurvey, is intended for students who are interested in developing a broad and practical knowledge of sustainable energy systems. It is an 18-month,120-ECTS (European Credit Transfer and Accumulation System) credit programme leading to an MSc degree in Sustainable Energy Science or in Sustainable Energy Engineering. Students study for 60 ECTS coursework credits and complete a 60 ECTS thesis.

The successful implementation of sustainable energy systems is an important challenge. REYST's emphasis is on students gaining a broad understanding of the environmental, social and economic forces driving the need for change, the technical possibilities for providing solutions, and the political and commercial means of bringing those solutions to fruition. They will also develop practical skills in a specific focus area.

Iceland is at the forefront of sustainable energy development: its electrical generation and heating come from renewable sources. REYST's industrial partners, which are leaders in their respective fields, have decades of experience in implementing and operating renewable energy systems. REYST offers students an excellent academic foundation, combined with exceptional access to real-life experience. They have the opportunity to do internships at Reykjavik Energy and Iceland Geosurvey, and to do their thesis work on projects that have immediate impact and relevance.

The REYST student body is culturally, professionally and educationally diverse. Students, who come from all corners of the world, have degrees in a wide range of subjects, including engineering, geophysics, economics, biology and management. Teaching is in English. Further information is on the website www.reyst.is.

Case study

R G Vishnu Menon (India) PhD in Business Administration
'When I'm asked "Why RU?", I say that you couldn't ask for a more fantastic experience than studying in the world's northernmost capital city in the vibrant and picturesque environment of Reykjavik University. The serene backdrop provides the perfect ambience for study and research. Moreover, the young and enthusiastic faculty at RU are easy to build a rapport with and RU organises numerous events, such as parties and tours to network with other students and explore beautiful Iceland. Another key aspect is the exposure students receive – I attended a poster presentation, an international conference and a seminar in Brussels, all within the first three months of joining RU!'

Verity Sharp (UK) MSc International Business
'I am in my first year at Reykjavik University studying for a Master's in International Business. Returning to education has been a big step for me, particularly as I left my BA degree in the UK dissatisfied with the higher education system. At RU things are different. The teachers know me as an individual and they provide first-class teaching. The programme content is excellent and with so many links to the international community I believe the programme here is opening many doors for me. Reykjavik University truly offers an exceptional and distinctive learning experience.'

Shishir Jayendra Patel (USA) BSc Computer Science
'Attending Reykjavik University has been a fantastic experience. I joined the university not knowing a lot about what I was getting myself into – and not knowing the language was the biggest task. I have found, however, that integrating into the student body was not as difficult as I had thought it would be. Everyone is very welcoming, and always willing to help, and this enables international students to feel at home. The academic side of RU is very demanding. The coursework may be a heavy load, but it proves that the university is looking to produce people who can adapt to any environment by providing the latest necessary skills, which are acquired through bookwork and group projects.'

Jacobs University

Jacobs University Bremen is Germany's premier, private, international, English-language university. 1,300 students from over 100 nations worldwide represent 75% of the student body. The campus is a vital, multicultural community united in the exciting and challenging work of shaping Jacobs University's mission: our goal is to prepare the leaders of tomorrow to responsibly meet global challenges.

In a suburban setting the 34-hectare green campus houses state-of-the-art laboratories, classroom facilities, a modern library and research centre, a cinema, theatre, café, Interfaith House, a new sport centre, including playing fields and a fitness centre, ensuring that there is always something interesting to do. All undergraduate students live in single rooms in residential colleges for all three years of their degree.

Jacobs University awards bachelor's, master's, and doctoral degrees in the natural sciences, engineering, the humanities and social sciences. The focus on transdisciplinarity allows students to declare their major at the beginning of the second year. They will be involved in hands-on research opportunities starting in the first year of study. The challenging three-year undergraduate programme will be complemented with a mandatory internship.

With a student:faculty ratio of 10:1, Jacobs offers excellent individualised attention. The constant intercultural exchange helps to develop global perspectives. Thus, students are uniquely well equipped for a career in an international area. Within three months of finishing their degree 90% of each graduating class successfully enters the workforce or a graduate school. Harvard, Yale, London School of Economics, Cambridge and Oxford have all been destinations of Jacobs' graduates wishing to continue their education.

Jacobs University is one of the top ranked universities in Germany according to the annual CHE rankings published in *Die Zeit*.

Inspired? Then find out more about Jacobs University at www.jacobs-university.de.

Case study

Sarah Islam (Bangladesh) Electrical and Computer Engineering (Class of 2012)

At Jacobs students come from 110 countries. What is your background?

'My schooling started in England where I was for a year. Then I came back to Bangladesh (where I was born) and studied through to 10th grade. I then went to America for a year as an exchange student.'

How did you hear about Jacobs University?

'The son of my father's friend attended Jacobs and praised it a lot (but warned me about the weather!). I chose Jacobs because of its reputation and high academic standing coupled with the unique international setting. No other university I looked at had this diversity. The scholarships offered by Jacobs are also substantial.'

Why did you choose your major?

'I chose electrical and computer engineering because I want to work in the power sector of Bangladesh which needs development.'

What do you like best about the campus?

'The campus is small enough that you can go anywhere in 10 minutes. The number of students is limited so even though it is not a huge area, there is a lot of space. It is 'quaint'. The colleges are very friendly places!'

What are the advantages of college life?

'The main advantage would be having a support system 24/7. Also, there is no "fitting in" to deal with here. Everyone is different, coming from different countries and cultures. It is just being yourself and enjoying the different and fun people.'

Eindhoven University of Technology (TU/e)

TU/e is a top Dutch university which has a unique Bachelor College and a strong Graduate School. Considered by the Study Guide to Universities 2012 as the best Dutch engineering and science university, studying at TU/e means that you study at a university offering top-quality education and internationally prominent research.

TU/e is a medium-sized university, where your studies are well supervised with plenty of personal contact and support from lecturers and staff. Experienced TU/e coaches are available to offer personal advice from the very beginning of your studies, from what major best suits you to how you can get the best out of your degree.

'Where innovation starts' is the TU/e slogan for a very good reason. The University lies in the technological heart of the Netherlands and boasts a good relationship with many high-tech companies and organizations. Students benefit from the opportunities these companies offer through assignments and internships.

Come to TU/e and be taught in English

All programmes offered by the computer-science department—the bachelor's programmes Web Science and Software Science, and all master's programmes—are taught in English.

Web Science is a program designed to emphasise the stable fundamentals of the internet as well as the role the internet plays in society.
For more information visit: www.tue.nl/webscience

Software Science is a course that aims to teach students to design and develop the underlying software systems of applications which are invisible but indispensable in modern society.
For more information visit: www.tue.nl/softwarescience

For more information on the master's and post-master's programmes, visit: www.tue.nl/graduateprograms/cs

Eindhoven University of Technology (TU/e)

Hrishikesh Salunkhe is a PhD student studying Embedded Systems at Eindhoven University of Technology (TU/e). Originally from India, Hrishikesh has moved to the Netherlands in order to study at one of the best technical universities in the world, TU/e.

'I was looking for really good universities in the field of Embedded Systems, and I quickly came across Eindhoven. Everybody here is really friendly. They have Dutch as their mother tongue, but they speak English – they really want you to be in a comfort zone.'

Strong ties to industry

Other strong factors in favour of the school are its strong ties to industry, the 'high tech campus', and working with professors who are very much involved in their fields.

'It's an industrial area with 80–90 companies that collaborate with the university. So there are great opportunities for research funding and, for me, it's really a thing of pride that I'm working with the people who are the best in the world.'

Student life

Student life isn't only about studying; it's also about being social and making friends.

'The campus is really lively. You have a lot of student committees – for example one where international people get together – like for birthdays or to eat food from different countries, or watching movies form different countries. So not only do you study, but you also get to enjoy life and understand different countries and cultures.'

Chapter 6
Studying in the USA

The USA is an increasingly attractive destination for UK students; in the academic year 2009/2010, 8,861 UK students went to the USA, with around 4,000 going for undergraduate-level study. More and more students seem to want to discover the appeal of the American higher education system; a system with a choice of over 4,500 universities and a broader, more flexible approach to university studies.

The education system

In the States, the terms university and college are generally used interchangeably. However, community colleges are different; they can only offer two-year associate degrees, rather than four-year bachelor's degrees.

Choosing where to study

When deciding where to apply, you need to consider which type of institution is right for you.

- **Public universities** are funded by the state and tend to have more students and lower fees. International students will end up paying more than state residents.
- **Private universities** tend to be campus-based, with better facilities and fewer students. They are funded by private donations, grants and tuition fees. Fees are higher, but the same fees are charged for all. More scholarships tend to be available.

- **Community colleges** offer associate degrees over two years (see opposite page), with the possibility of transferring to a university to top up to a full bachelor's degree. They are often cheaper and less competitive.

The Ivy League is made up of eight prestigious private universities and colleges in the north-east of the USA. It started out as a sports league, rather than any kind of elite group or ranking system. For this reason, many top universities from across the country are not in the Ivy League, including Berkeley, which is a public university, and Stanford, which is on the west coast.

American degrees are made up of a range of types of courses.

- **Core** (or general education), providing the compulsory foundation for university study. Students will often be required to select from a broad range of courses including sciences, history, maths, English composition and literature and so on.
- **Major** courses, your main subject area; choose from options like English, engineering or history.
- **Minor** courses, taken in a secondary subject or allowing you to specialise within your main subject area. You could minor in a foreign language or consider adding a computer science minor to a maths major.
- **Academic track**, a group of courses focused on a specific topic within a major; a student majoring in computer science could select a track in computer systems, for example.

Some universities offer co-operative education programmes, made up of paid work experience, rather like a sandwich course in the UK. In other cases, unpaid internships may offer degree credit.

Finding a course

You can use College Board (undergraduate), www.collegeboard. com, or College Navigator (undergraduate and postgraduate), http://nces.ed.gov/collegenavigator, to search for courses at public, private or community colleges. EducationUSA features a list of other college or course search sites on its '5 steps to study' web page, www.educationusa.info/5_steps_to_study/.

Transfers

It is possible to transfer between universities. Transfers would normally take place after **freshman** year (Year 1), but (since you need a minimum of two years at a university to graduate) any later than **sophomore** year (Year 2) could prove tricky.

The academic year runs from mid-August or early September to late May or early June.

Associate degrees

Associate degrees like Associate of Arts (AA) or Associate of Science (AS) are two year programmes of general studies along with foundation courses in a chosen subject (a major or field of concentration). The qualifications often relate to vocational areas like hospitality management or health sciences. The programme might include core and concentration courses, **electives**, practical work, fieldwork and supervised study. They are broadly equivalent to the first year of UK undergraduate study. After completion, students may wish to transfer to a US bachelor's degree by completing an additional two years of study.

Students who are only applying with GCSE qualifications could apply for an associate degree. Certain vocational qualifications might be accepted by community colleges, but not by the more competitive universities.

American college year names

Year 1   Freshman Year
Year 2   Sophomore Year
Year 3   Junior Year
Year 4   Senior Year

Bachelor's degrees

Bachelor's degrees generally take four years to complete, although there are some five-year courses in architecture, sciences and engineering. A US bachelor's degree is comparable in level to a British bachelor's degree. Unlike in the UK, where you choose your subject before you apply, you can apply for an undecided major, and decide on your chosen subject at the end of sophomore (or second) year. This has more in common with the Scottish system of education than with the rest of the UK. Much of the first, and some of the second year is spent on a range of introductory courses. Some of this core curriculum will relate to subjects you may wish to make your main subject choice (or major). For example, if you are considering majoring in psychology, you might opt for maths and quantitative reasoning and social and behavioural sciences as your core subjects.

> 66 I have had one-to-one support from the international student advisor who was fantastic in setting up my schedule and what I was going to study. 99
> *Stuart Bramley, Scottsdale Community College, USA*

Entry requirements vary, but most would require a minimum of five GCSEs or Standard Grades at C or above including maths and English. You would need to show that you are completing advanced-level study; the universities will be able to check your attainment from your academic transcript and any admissions tests you sit. Competitive universities will be looking for three A levels or equivalent. Less competitive universities may consider vocational qualifications, like a BTEC Extended Diploma, a vocational course broadly equivalent to three A levels. For more information on applying, see the following section.

Honours degrees

Gaining an honours degree in the USA tends to indicate that the student has defended an undergraduate thesis (or piece of original research) known in the UK as a dissertation. Confusingly, a degree with honours can also mean that someone has achieved with particular academic merit, although this is more usually known in the USA as *Cum laude* (with honour), *Magna cum laude* (with great honour) or *Summa cum laude* (with highest honour).

Graduate school

What we know as postgraduate education in the UK is described as graduate education or grad school in the USA. Master's degrees and PhDs gained in the USA are comparable to British master's degrees and PhDs. Certain subjects that you could start at undergraduate level in the UK can only be taken at graduate level in the USA; these include medicine and law. Pre-med and pre-law programmes are available at undergraduate level, although these programmes aren't a mandatory requirement for medical or law school.

Applying

The application process for undergraduate and postgraduate courses has some similarities to the UK system, although there is no admissions service like UCAS to co-ordinate applications. For the most part, applications are made direct to the chosen institution, although some universities use the Common Application for undergraduate programmes; see the opposite page for more information.

As part of the application process, you will be required to send detailed academic records and official course information for qualifications you have completed. You may be required to submit your academic documents to an organisation that can convert your qualifications to a comparable level of study in the USA. Your university will give you further details of which organisation to use or, for a list of approved agencies, try the National Association of Credential Evaluation Services (NACES), www.naces.org.

Undergraduate applications

The timescale for applications is similar to UCAS, although there is a separate system if you are applying for a sports scholarship.

After Christmas in your first year at sixth form or college (Y13 in Northern Ireland or S5 in Scotland), you will need to start researching degree programmes and universities. It is suggested that you narrow down your choice to around five or six universities, due to the time and costs involved.

Most applications comprise of:

- application form
- fee (around $50 to $100 (£32 to £64) per university)
- admissions test scores
- a few essays (of around 500 to 750 words)
- transcript (details of your academic performance)
- two or three recommendations

- financial statement
- possibility of an interview.

Each of these components will be explained in more detail below.

You will be applying to the university as a whole, so admissions staff will decide your fate, not academic staff from your chosen department. They will be looking at more than just success at A level; GCSEs, AS levels, your passion for learning, your love for your subject (if you have decided on a major) and you as a person will all be considered.

Although you can apply for an undecided major, you will normally apply to a particular school within the university, for example the School of Arts, School of Engineering or School of Management.

Application forms

From 1 August, the Common Application becomes available at www.commonapp.org. This is used by around 450 universities, although each university involved still retains its own deadlines, administration fees and requirements. All other universities require direct applications, so you may have a number of forms to complete. There tend to be more sections to complete and more space available than on the UCAS application, so it can result in quite a lot of work. Most applications are similar, so you will not have to start completely from scratch with each one. You will be able to copy and paste information, as long as you remember to amend and target it each time.

Universities tend to offer separate deadlines for early action applications, often sometime in November. Early action applications are to one university only; this demonstration of commitment can have its benefits for consideration by the university and for scholarships. There are regular admissions deadlines a little later, often in December or January. Check individual institutions for full details.

Undergraduate admissions tests

You will need to check whether an admissions test will be necessary. Many universities will be looking for both good grades and strong admissions test scores; this is particularly so if you are applying for academic merit-based scholarships (see Help with finances on page 172). Where an admission test is required, the amount of importance placed upon the test scores varies between universities.

Most universities ask for the American College Test (ACT) or the Scholastic Assessment Test (SAT) for undergraduate-level study; both tests are designed to assess academic potential. If the university accepts both, you will be able to choose which test to sit. Although the tests are both well-recognised and essentially achieve the same objective, the tests themselves are different and you may find one will suit you more than the other. The SAT originally set out to measure aptitude, while the ACT was achievement-based, although both have changed since their inception.

The ACT includes more questions, so you end up with less time per question; it includes English, reading, science and higher maths. It comprises a single test, which may be more convenient, but is only available in limited locations across the UK. For the more competitive universities, you are likely to have to complete a supplementary 30-minute writing section (in addition to the nearly three-hour-long ACT test). It costs around $60 (£38), plus $15 (£9.67) for the written section.

The SAT comprises a reasoning test of nearly four hours, plus two or three subject tests for the more competitive universities. The test is widely available in the UK, but both tests are taken on different dates. It costs around $80 (£51) for the reasoning test and $62 (£40) for each subject test.

It is essential to be prepared for these tests. Take a look at www.fulbright.co.uk/study-in-the-usa/undergraduate-study/ admissions-tests/preparing-for-the-sat-act and www.collegeboard. org to help you prepare.

Sitting a test in early autumn of year 13 in England and Wales, Y14 in Northern Ireland or S6 in Scotland is ideal, as it gives you time to re-sit, if necessary. Some candidates choose to take their first test as early as the previous spring. Candidates need to register sometime between spring and mid-September. It is worth registering early as places can quickly fill up. You can register and find a testing centre through the ACT website, www.act.org, and the SAT website, http://sat.collegeboard.org.

Essays

Essays are likely to be based on your response to specific questions set by the university; make sure you answer the questions fully and directly. They may want to find out about your skills and personality traits; why you want to study at this university, what are your goals and what inspires you? Although you might choose to write on a subject related to your area of interest, you do not normally have to do so. The Fulbright Commission (www.fulbright.co.uk/study-in-the-usa/ undergraduate-study/applying/essays) has examples, video tips and useful handouts on this subject.

Sample questions for the common application essay (University of Virginia).

- Discuss some issue of personal, local, national or international concern and its importance to you.
- Indicate a person who has had a significant influence on you and describe that influence.
- Describe a character in fiction, a historical figure or a creative work that has had an influence on you, and explain that influence.

Transcripts

The transcript should include predicted grades from your current qualifications, but also your progress from year 10 (Y11 in Northern Ireland or S3 in Scotland) onwards. It could include GCSE or Standard Grades, details of any exams taken since then (AS levels and so on), results of mock exams or other internal assessments and any academic honours achieved. Where relevant, ask your school or college to include explanations for any anomalies in your academic record. Qualifications may also need to be explained and details of the institution incorporated.

The format of the transcript is generally chronological. It should be around a page in length and produced on official headed paper. You will need to work with your school or college to help them prepare this, directing them to sample transcripts, such as those on the Fulbright Commission website (www.fulbright.co.uk).

On the application form, you'll be asked for your GPA. The Grade Point Average cannot be officially converted from UK qualifications, so you should leave this section blank.

Recommendations

You will need to arrange two or three letters of reference or recommendations from staff who know you well; follow your chosen university's guidelines on who to ask. The restrained and often modest tone taken in a UCAS reference might not be enough for a US university. Recommendations from US schools tend to be far more detailed and far more positive, so you will need to prepare your referee to really sell you. Refer potential referees to the Fulbright Commission website for tips and sample letters, www.fulbright.co.uk/study-in-the-usa/undergraduate-study/applying/reference-letters.

The EducationUSA website (www.educationusa.info) explains why you might choose to waive your right to see a copy of the recommendation: 'A recommendation form may include a waiver where you can relinquish your right to see what is written about you. If this option is offered, most admissions officers prefer you to waive your right so that recommenders may feel more comfortable when writing their evaluations. Admissions officers usually interpret waived recommendations as more honest.'

Financial statement

How will you fund your studies in the USA? Your university will want to know, so you will need to complete any requests for evidence. You can use the evidence again when applying for a visa. You will need to show that you can at least cover the first year's costs, maybe even the costs for the length of the whole course. If you need financial assistance, you should include how much will be required. In most cases, a 'need-blind' admissions system means that your application will not be affected by this evidence.

Interview

These days, the internet and Skype are typically used for interviewing. You may be surprised to find yourself being interviewed by an ex-student. Alternatively, the interview may be with a member of admissions staff. They may come to the UK or may ask you to go to the States, in which case you could enquire about help with travel expenses.

You could be asked why you have chosen this university, how you will contribute and why you intend to study in the USA. They will want to know about your subject interests, whether you have any ideas about your major or what your strengths and weaknesses are.

To prepare, you should look over the research you did when choosing this university. You can read over the essays you sent and look at how you can expand upon what was written. You should prepare questions to ask of the interviewer, but make sure any questions aren't already answered in the university's prospectus or website.

Offers

Early action applicants get an answer in December or January, while regular applicants hear later in the spring. The response could be one of three options: accepted, wait list or not accepted. Those accepted can choose to accept, decline or defer. (Deferring is rare, so you should always check the process with your university. Even if your university agrees, any offers for funding might not also be deferred.) A deposit of around $500 (£322) will secure your place.

If you are placed on a waiting list, there is still a possibility that you will be offered a place; follow any instructions you receive about the waiting list process and keep your fingers crossed.

Your offer won't be conditional, but it is still important to work hard and do well. You may gain university credit or advanced standing from good UK qualifications.

Applying for graduate school

As with undergraduate admissions, students apply direct to their chosen universities. The Fulbright Commission suggests restricting applications to between four and six institutions.

The details of deadline dates, entry requirements and application fees will vary, although most will require some of the following:

- application form
- fee (around $50 to $100 (£32 to £64) per university)
- admissions test scores
- a few essays (of around 500 to 750 words)
- **research statement**
- transcript (details of your academic performance)
- two or three recommendations
- possibility of an interview.

Each application may be different but, rather like a job application, you should be able to adapt the information you provide, rather than starting from scratch each time.

Most universities will be looking for at least a 2:2 from UK undergraduate study, with the more competitive universities looking for considerably more. They will be looking at your all-round offer, not just academic achievements, but also the way you demonstrate a good understanding of your chosen university and how this matches you as an individual. US universities are also keen to know about your involvement in extracurricular activities. Contact the universities directly to discuss their requirements.

Much of the information in the previous section on applying for undergraduate study will also apply to postgraduate applications (see page 162). Notable differences include the research statement and the different admissions tests.

Research statement

The research statement allows you to outline your areas of interest, specialism and plans for how and why you intend to complete your research. Here are some of the key points that you need to consider when writing a research statement.

- Sum up your current plans for research, understanding that they may well change as you refine your ideas or as other developments occur.
- Relate your plans to your chosen university department and professors.
- Demonstrate your intellectual skills, but without alienating the admissions staff who may be considering your application.

Graduate admissions tests

Most postgraduate options require an admission test and there are a number of different tests to consider:

- Dental Admissions Test (DAT), www.ada.org/dat.aspx
- Graduate Management Admissions Test (GMAT), www. mba.com
- Graduate Record Exam (GRE), www.ets.org/gre/
- Law School Admissions Test (LSAT), http://lsat.org/
- Medical College Admission Test (MCAT), https://www. aamc.org/students/applying/mcat

The cost of these tests can be quite substantial, with DAT costing $320 (£206) and MCAT $305 (£196). Some tests are available across the country, with others restricted to London and the DAT currently only being tested in the USA.

How the tests are used also varies, with some tests being a central factor in a successful application, while other tests are considered along with a variety of different aspects. In some cases, looking at how your scores compare to last year's averages can help to indicate your chances of success.

Preparation is vital, as the system tends to rely quite heavily on multiple choice testing. Remember that you will be competing with US students who are used to this style of testing, so you need to know what to expect. See the individual test websites for sample papers or use the Fulbright Commission's 'Preparing for Admission Exams' page at www.fulbright.co.uk/study-in-the-usa/postgraduate-study/admissions-tests/preparation.

Visas

If you plan to study in the USA and you aren't a US citizen or a permanent resident in the USA, you will need a visa. You should apply for this at a US Embassy or US Consulate before you leave the UK. There are two visa categories, F-1 Student Visa and J-1 Exchange Visitor Visa; F-1 is for students undertaking a full-time programme in the USA, while J-1 is for those on **study abroad programmes** or exchanges. If in doubt, your university will tell you which one to apply for. There are differences in restrictions on these two visas; whether you can work off-campus, for example (see page 176).

> After you receive your visa you will need it upon entry to the USA and then again for opening accounts etc. After this you should store it carefully. Be aware of things that may impact on it, for example, if you decide to travel or get a job.
>
> *Simon McCabe, University of*
> *Missouri, USA*

Once you have been offered a place at a university and provided evidence as to how you will fund the first year of your studies, your institution will prepare a Form I-20 (F-1 visa) or Form DS-2019 (J-1 visa); you will need this to apply for your visa. The university will also send instructions as to how to apply. The process will involve a visa interview at the US Embassy in London or the US Consulate in Belfast, as well as completion of an online SEVIS I-901 form (requiring a $140 fee) and an online visa form (requiring a $180/£116 fee for J-1 or $200/£129 fee for F-1).

If your application is successful, you will normally be admitted for the duration of your student status. You should check any visa restrictions and follow them to the letter, as breach of these conditions is an offence.

Costs and help with finances

Tuition fees in the USA can be considerably higher than across the rest of the world. However, weigh this up against a strong tradition of financial aid and things might not always be as expensive as first anticipated.

Costs

According to the College Board (www.collegeboard.org), the following average tuition fees were reported for 2010/2011:

- two-year, Public Community Colleges: $2,713 (£1,750)
- four-year, Public Institutions (out-of-state students): $19,595 (£12,641)
- four-year, Private Institutions: $27,293 (£17,608).

You should allow in the region of $10,000 (£6,451) per year for accommodation, food, books and materials, travel and so on. This amount will vary depending on where you live and the type of lifestyle you lead. Universities will provide an idea of local living costs on their websites.

The USA comes in at number 29 of 83 countries on a cost of living ranking from Numbeo (www.numbeo.com). This suggests its living costs are more reasonable than the UK, Canada, Australia, New Zealand and much of Northern Europe.

If you are looking at ways to make US education more affordable, you could consider taking a year or two at a community college before transferring to a university.

Research carried out by EducationUSA reveals that in 2009/2010, more than 900 universities supported their international students in the following ways: some awarded amounts of over $10,000 (£6,451); some offered options costing under $15,000 (£9,677) per year (including fees, accommodation, travel etc); while others brought costs below $15,000 (£9,677) with financial aid or scholarships.

Help with finances

While you cannot access the UK student loans and grants for overseas study, there may be some alternative options available. You should be researching universities and investigating funding concurrently, since your choice of university will impact on your options for certain scholarships or financial aid. Start early and consider that support will often be pulled from a number of sources:

- scholarships from universities
- scholarships from external bodies

- sports scholarships
- savings or personal loans from the UK
- financial aid.

Much of the additional funding you may be applying for comes directly from US universities. Scholarships are allocated based on a range of criteria: merit, achievements, financial need, talents or personal background (country of origin, gender or ethnicity). Use the admissions or financial aid pages on the university website to find out which institutions offer scholarships to UK students. Keep in mind that, even if you are lucky enough to get a scholarship, it is unlikely to cover all your costs.

The amount of financial aid varies between colleges. For example, if you have the brains to get into Harvard and your family income is under $60,000 (£38,709) per year, then you would not have to pay anything. Further financial aid is awarded on a sliding scale for family income of over $60,000.

> You can speed up your studies, and thereby reduce some of your costs, by taking additional courses each semester or gaining credit over the summer break.

Sports scholarships are a highly competitive option and you will need to start the process even earlier than for a mainstream application. Applicants must meet and maintain academic standards, while also having the sporting talent to participate at varsity (inter-university) level. Scholarships are awarded for a range of sports, with opportunities for UK students in soccer, golf, athletics or swimming, for example.

Certain sporting associations will require scores over a particular level on SATs or ACTs. You can make contact with university coaches directly or use the services of an agent, who will often charge a fee. Both EducationUSA and the Fulbright Commission have handouts on their websites taking you through each option.

There are a range of external bodies that offer scholarships, each with their own specifications and deadlines. Try this web page for more details of organisations you might want to contact: www. fulbright.co.uk/study-in-the-usa/undergraduate-study/funding/ external-funding-bodies.

The following websites will help you get started on your search for funding:

- www.educationusa.info/pages/students/finance.php
- www.edupass.org/finaid/databases.phtml
- www.iefa.org/
- www.internationalscholarships.com/

Cultural differences

If you have watched enough Hollywood films, you may feel you already know the USA. You may have heard of Thanksgiving and Spring Break and you probably have some ideas about campus life. Therefore you might not expect to experience culture shock when leaving for this western, English-speaking country. Although the changes won't necessarily be too extreme, it may still take a little while to adjust and feelings of homesickness and uncertainty are normal.

Meeting new people and making friends is important to help you start to feel at home. It may be tempting to stick with other international students, but if you want to get to know the real America, you will need to meet some Americans. As a nation, they are much more open than the Brits, so introduce yourself to hall mates and classmates or get involved with activities.

Drinking is less of a way of life than in the UK. The legal age is 21 and many university events, and even whole campuses, are dry.

Working while studying

Full-time students on a Student Visa (F-1) can work 20 hours per week on campus. You must have all appropriate paperwork, including SEVIS I-20, passport and Social Security Card – speak to your university for more information. Campus jobs might include library, cafeteria or office work. It makes sense to wait until you have had time to adjust to your new country before you start looking for work. Remember that breaking employment law could lead to deportation.

Paid, off-campus employment is permissible through Curricular Practical Training (CPT), but it must be an integral part of your degree curriculum. If you are interested in CPT, look out for courses where an internship or practicum (practical work in a particular field) is required. Technical courses, like engineering, or vocational courses, like special education, might require this type of experience.

It is possible to gain work experience during your studies in the USA and to work for up to one year on an Optional Practical Training (OPT) scheme; it is possible to do this during your studies, although most students opt to do it afterwards. The work is paid and at a professional level but must be related to your field of studies as listed on your SEVIS I-20. You will also need permission from the US Citizen and Immigration Services.

If you get a job with a recognised international organisation, you can work if it's relevant to your studies, even if it isn't a requirement of your course. You can still opt for Optional Practical Training afterwards, regardless of the length of your work with the international organisation. Your university will be able to tell you more.

Staying on after study

Once your course has finished, unless you have further study or Optional Practical Training lined up, it will be time to return to the UK. You normally get 60 days' grace at the end of your studies, which you could spend tying up your affairs or seeing some of this vast country.

Occasionally, some students get job offers which mean that they can stay on and eventually apply for a green card, giving the right of permanent residence. Alternatively, if close family are permanent residents of the USA, they may be able to sponsor you to stay on permanently. Don't go to the States banking on the chance to stay; these opportunities are the exception, rather than the rule. You can find out more at the website for the US Citizenship and Immigration Services, www. uscis.gov.

Pros and cons

Pros

- Some of the most highly rated universities in the world.
- More international students choose the USA than anywhere else.
- Opportunities for financial aid or scholarships for international students.

- Great facilities and campuses.
- English-speaking country.

Cons

- Few opportunities to stay on permanently.
- High university tuition fees.

Chapter 7
Studying in Canada

If you're looking to get more for your money than in the UK and considering a country with a good quality of life where you may be able to stay on afterwards, Canada has a lot to offer.

The education system

The education system in Canada is run by a separate Ministry of Education in each province or territory. Each region has consistent standards and it is fairly easy to move between them. Courses are taught in English or French; some institutions teach in both languages.

The academic year runs from September to May and is divided into two semesters. Fall term runs from September to December and winter term follows from January to May. Some institutions offer a trimester system, with an additional summer term starting from May onwards, although there may be more limited programme choice at this time. Although it is possible to join courses in the second (and sometimes the third) term, September intake is the most common.

University study

More than 10,000 undergraduate and postgraduate degree programmes are available at a range of public and private (not-for-profit) universities and university degree level colleges. The majority of universities in Canada are public. Canada's education system is considered to be of high quality, with investment in research and development at universities in Canada almost twice that of any other G8 nation. Canada can also boast nine universities in the 2011/2012 Times Higher Education World University Rankings Top 200. Bachelor's, master's and doctoral degrees are comparable in level to those from the UK.

How to find a course

The official Study in Canada portal is a good starting point for your research; it features a course finder and links to information from the 10 provinces and three territories, as well as links to the individual institutions, www.educationau-incanada.ca.

The Association of Universities and Colleges of Canada (www.aucc.ca) features a course search, as well as university profiles, facts and figures and information on quality assurance.

Accreditation and quality

You can check that your chosen institution is accredited by using the Directory of Universities, Colleges and Schools in the Provinces and Territories of Canada. You can find this at www.cicic.ca (Canadian Information Centre for International Credentials). The listing includes all public and accredited institutions, as well as some private establishments.

Undergraduate study

Bachelor's degrees from Canada take three or four years to complete. In some cases, an honours degree is part of the degree programme; in other cases, it is taken as an extra year of study. You will generally be looking at four years of study for an honours degree.

Four-year applied bachelor's degrees offer a more vocational option, combining academic study with the development of the

more practical skills needed for employment. If you're looking
to incorporate work experience, co-op programmes are similar
to sandwich courses in the UK, providing the opportunity to
work as well as gain academic credentials. It is worth noting that
certain competitive fields may not always be widely available to
international students; your university will be able to advise you
of any issues.

Differences from education in the UK

A key difference in Canadian education is that the degrees tend
to be much more general than you would expect in the UK,
particularly when compared to England, Wales and Northern
Ireland. Although there will be certain programmes you must
study to achieve your 'major', you will have the option to study a
range of additional subjects. For the first two years you might be
choosing programmes from general sciences or general arts, for
example, before starting to specialise.

> **66** In Canada, we have **midterm** exams and many
> smaller assignments due throughout the year.
> School also goes all year round if you want it to, although
> most people don't take classes in the summer semester. You
> have to obtain a certain amount of credits to gain your
> degree and each class you take is worth a certain amount of
> credits (usually three). **99**
>
> *Alex Warren, University of British*
> *Columbia, Canada*

Higher education in Canada takes place in universities,
university colleges and community colleges. Some universities
are **research intensive**, with others focusing purely on teaching,

in contrast to the UK, where all universities tend to carry out both teaching and research. The institution website (or the institution's staff) should reveal what type of institution it is.

Associate degrees

Some students may choose to take their first and second year at a community college, studying for an associate degree, before transferring to a university to achieve a bachelor's degree. Colleges tend to offer applied (rather than purely academic) studies, smaller classes (university classes can be large, particularly in years one and two) and lower tuition fees. There is some snobbery and colleges are sometimes considered to be the second choice to university. Associate degrees take two years on a full-time basis and are broadly equivalent to a Certificate of HE in the UK.

Entry requirements

Much like the UK, each university sets its own admissions requirements and publicises the minimum qualifications required. High school graduation in Canada is at a similar level to A levels or Advanced Highers in Scotland; universities will generally be looking for applicants educated to this level. Community colleges may have slightly lower entry requirements. Your institution will be able to tell you more, including whether they have any additional requirements, for example for competitive or specialist subjects.

If you intend to study in French, the institution will talk to you about the level of French they require and whether an assessment of your skills will be necessary.

Postgraduate study

Postgraduate courses are available at some, but not all, universities in Canada and include master's and doctoral degrees. Postgraduate study in Canada includes coursework, although less than at undergraduate level, alongside research. The courses tend to be based around seminars and will involve large amounts of structured reading, particularly in the early years.

Most master's degrees take two years to complete and don't always require completion of a thesis. Doctoral degrees (for example PhDs) last between four and seven years, with a dissertation forming an essential component of the qualification. It is sometimes possible to move straight from an undergraduate honours degree to a doctoral degree. In these cases, the doctoral degree will often incorporate the master's degree.

> What we know as 'postgraduate study' in the UK is more commonly known as 'graduate study' in Canada and the USA.

For those intending to a follow a regulated profession like law, medicine or social work, a licence to practise is granted following success in academic study and a relevant internship.

Entry requirements

Institutions will normally require an honours degree for progression to postgraduate study, although some exceptions are made for those with substantial work experience. Three-year degrees from the UK (and other parts of the European Higher Education Area) should meet the general entry requirements for postgraduate study in Canada.

Academic recognition

Your chosen institution may already know and understand the qualification you are applying with; in which case, they may accept your certificates without further evaluation. If the qualification is unfamiliar, or they are less experienced at dealing with international qualifications, you may need to pay to have your qualification evaluated. Talk to the admissions staff to see whether evaluation is required, as you may save yourself some money if you don't need this service. The Canadian Centre for International Credentials (www.cicic.ca) will provide further information on how to proceed.

Applying

Your first step when applying should be to contact the international office requesting application documentation. They should send you information about the application procedure and timescale, along with requirements for the evaluation of qualifications, the costs of study and the visa application processes.

Alberta, British Columbia and Ontario each have a centralised application service, while Québec has a number of different regional systems. You will find that many individual institutions require direct application. Applications may be paper-based or online. Applications will incur a fee, often well in excess of the £21 required by UCAS. If you are applying to a number of universities in various provinces, you may have to pay more than once. Remember to factor in this cost when working out the costs of study. Careful research and narrowing down your choices should help to reduce these costs, and the additional work required by multiple applications.

Application deadline dates vary between provinces and between individual institutions. International applicants are normally required to apply between December and early spring for September start, in the autumn for January start and around January for start dates in the summer. Graduate application deadlines may be earlier, particularly for the more competitive courses.

Start planning for your application a good year in advance. Bear in mind that evaluation of qualifications, the need to sit admissions tests and the time taken for international post may slow the process down considerably. You should expect a decision around four or five months after the deadline date, although this will also vary between institutions.

The application form

The application form itself is likely to be quite a small part of the application process, requiring basic information about the applicant's:

- personal details
- contact details
- education
- test scores
- relevant professional experience (where applicable)
- referees.

Further documents required in support of an application could include:

- transcript
- **letter of intent/statement of purpose**
- essay or sample of writing
- letters of reference
- proof of immigration status.

A CV, medical form and portfolio may be required for certain courses. Similarly, a criminal records check will only be required in certain cases.

There will be an initial deadline date for the application and a later date for the provision of the supporting documentation. Some institutions won't consider an application until all documents are received, so send all documents promptly to improve your chances.

Transcript

A transcript is an academic record produced by your school, college or university. It might include details of your education and progress from year 10 in England and Wales, year 11 in Northern Ireland or S3 in Scotland. It will include exam and mock exam results, internal assessment results and predicted grades; it should include any special awards or recommendation, as well as an explanation of any problems or anomalies in your educational attainment.

Letter of intent or statement of purpose

This is a key part of the application and may determine whether you are accepted. Use the statement to explain your interest, any relevant experience and what you hope to achieve with the qualification. You need to demonstrate your suitability and your potential. Try to analyse your experiences and remember to back up any claims you make about your strengths with examples. Explain any discrepancies or gaps in your education.

At postgraduate level, you should incorporate an outline of the research you intend to undertake. Consider what interests you about this area of work, how you intend to approach the research and illustrate how the research will fit in with the focus of the department.

The statement needs to be well-written and free from spelling and grammatical errors. Two typed A4 pages should be sufficient.

Letters of reference

A letter of reference should be a positive document that provides details of your skills, strengths and achievements; a detailed, targeted letter is much more helpful than a general one. You will need to find two or three academic staff who know you well and can comment on your capabilities and really sell you.

Provide your referee with details of the courses you are applying for, along with a copy of your statement and transcript. You could suggest some of the key skills you would like them to draw attention to.

The referee will need to illustrate their own academic competence and background. The referee should provide specific examples of your strengths, since any claims should be backed up by relevant evidence. It may be useful for your referee to compare your achievements and skills to others that he or she has taught.

Give your referees around one month to compile the letters. It is helpful to gently follow them up to check that the letters have been completed. Thank them for their efforts; you may need to use their services again.

Tips, sample references and standard reference forms are available on university websites. See the University of British Columbia, www.grad.ubc.ca/prospective-students/application-admission/letters-reference, and McGill University, www.mcgill.ca/law-admissions/undergraduates/admissions/documents/#LETTERS, for some examples.

Admissions tests

Canada does not have a standardised university entrance exam; universities have their own admissions requirements. In most cases, UK students shouldn't need to take admissions tests for undergraduate courses.

Entrance exams required by Canadian graduate schools include the GRE (Graduate Record Examination), which can be taken across the world (www.ets.org/gre). It is available as a computer-based test in the UK and costs US$170 (£109) when taken outside Canada. Other tests include the Graduate Management Admissions Test (GMAT) for business studies (www.mba.com), LSAT for Law School (http://lsat.org/) and MCAT for Medical School (www.aamc.org).

Different universities use the results from these tests in different ways. In some cases, the result will be a deciding factor; in others, the result will be just one of a number of considerations. Ask your chosen institution how they use the results and what kinds of scores previous applicants have achieved.

You are likely to do better in these tests if you are prepared for the style of questioning and any time limits for completion. Books and courses are available to help you prepare. You can take tests like the GRE more than once, but the costs can end up being quite substantial if you do so.

What next?

If you are successful in gaining a place at a Canadian college or university, you will be provided with a letter of acceptance. The next step will be to apply for a study permit.

Visas

A study permit is required for anyone who will be studying for more than six months in the country; you will need to apply to the Canadian High Commission in London. To gain a study permit, you will need to prove that you can pay your tuition fees and living costs of around C$10,000 (£6,172) per year, although this can vary according to where you will be living and studying. You will also need to be in good health and without a criminal record. Follow all instructions carefully and allow around 10 weeks for processing. There is a processing fee of C$125 (£77).

There are different immigration requirements if you study in Québec, where a certificat d'acceptation du Québec (CAQ) from the Immigration Service of Québec is required prior to entry to Canada. See www.immigration-quebec.gouv.qc.ca/ en/immigrate-settle/students/index.html.

If your university or college welcomes lots of international students, the staff should be experienced in supporting applicants through the immigration procedures.

Further information on the procedures and how to apply can be found at www.cic.gc.ca/english/study/index.asp.

Costs and help with finances

Canada promotes itself as being more affordable for international students than the USA and Australia.

Costs

Tuition fees across the provinces and territories of Canada vary. According to Imagine Studying in Canada (the Council of Ministers of Education) university tuition fees range from C$8,000 to C$26,000 (£4,938–£16,049) per year, with college fees of between C$5,500 and C$15,000 (£3,395–£9,259) per year. In 2009/2010 international students paid undergraduate fees averaging $15,674 (£9,675) (www.statcan.gc.ca).

> **❝** The cost of study has been a lot more expensive but now that the fees in the UK have gone up the difference is much less. The fees are approximately C$8,000 (£4,938) per semester. I also received an entrance scholarship and a second scholarship in my second year. **❞**
>
> *Alex Warren, University of British Columbia, Canada*

Some research-based postgraduate study is subsidised and the fees can be lower than undergraduate fees. To calculate more specific costs for the courses and institutions you are interested in, the Imagine Studying in Canada website has a useful cost calculator at http://w01.educationau-incanada.ca/index. aspx?action=cost-cout&lang=eng.

> The British Columbia Council for International Education (BCCIE) suggests annual costs for tuition and living of around C$15,000 to C$30,000 (£9,259 to £18,518) per year. Your university will be able to provide you with estimates of local living expenses.

To compare the cost of living in Canada to the rest of the world, try the Numbeo Cost of Living Ranking at www.numbeo.com. Canada is ranked number 19 of 83 countries, suggesting it is cheaper than the UK, Australia and New Zealand.

Help with finances

If you're looking for a scholarship to help offset the costs of international study, be prepared to start your research early, more than a year ahead. Consider how you will support yourself, as scholarships are limited, highly competitive and may not cover the full costs of your studies.

Talk to your chosen university about any scholarships they offer and take a look at the Canadian Government's website as a starting point, www.scholarships-bourses.gc.ca/scholarships-bourses/index.aspx?view=d.

Scholarships include the Canadian Commonwealth Scholarship Program, Vanier Canada Graduate Scholarships and Trudeau Scholarships. There are more opportunities for postgraduate than undergraduate study.

Other sources of information include:

- www.cbie.ca/english/scholarship/non_canadians.htm
- www.acu.ac.uk/study_in_the_commonwealth/study
- www.ScholarshipsCanada.com

Cultural differences

Canada is considered to be a tolerant and multicultural society and it welcomes students from across the world. Canadian culture shares much with its neighbour, the USA, but there are differences. The province of Québec is French speaking and culturally quite different from the rest of the nation. Parts of Canada show a particularly British influence, including Toronto and Victoria.

Adjusting to the sheer size of Canada can be a shock, as well as getting used to the long, cold winter in much of the country.

Citizenship and Immigration Canada has some helpful information on culture shock, as well as on adjusting to life and the weather in Canada at www.cic.gc.ca/english/newcomers/after-life-shock.asp.

Working while studying

Full-time degree-level students can work on campus at their university or college without any special permission. You will need a work permit to work off campus; the permit allows you to work up to 20 hours per week during term-time and full-time in the official holidays. If you are taking a spouse or partner with you, they may be able to work, subject to medical clearance.

Citizenship and Immigration Canada should tell you all you need to know about working while studying, co-op programmes and internships, and working after graduation, www.cic.gc.ca/english/study/work.asp.

Staying on after study

The Canadian authorities have a number of programmes that allow students to stay on in Canada after completion of their studies. Remember that these schemes change from time to time and may even have changed by the time you complete your studies.

Postgraduate work permit program

Graduating students can apply for a permit of up to three years, depending on the length of their studies, see www.cic.gc.ca/english/study/work-postgrad.asp.

Canadian experience class

Graduating students have the opportunity to apply to stay on in Canada permanently; you will need to meet various conditions

including at least one year's Canadian work experience, see www.
cic.gc.ca/english/immigrate/cec/index.asp.

Provincial nominee program

If you are considered to offer the skills, education and experience
to make an immediate economic contribution to your province,
you may be able to gain residence under this scheme, www.cic.
gc.ca/english/immigrate/provincial/index.asp.

If you are leaving Canada, you can still remain connected
through the Global Canadian Alumni Network. The nearest
Canadian Embassy or High Commission will be able to tell
you more.

Pros and cons

Pros

- Good quality of education.
- High investment in research and development.
- Opportunities to stay and work after graduating.
- Possibility of emigrating after graduating.

Cons

- Certain competitive fields may not always be widely
  available to international students.
- Different systems in place in the different provinces.

Seneca College of Applied Arts and Technology

Seneca

At Seneca, thousands of students live their dreams every day by pursuing some of the most exciting careers in the world. Our award-winning programmes range from business and technology to fashion arts, computer science, graphic design, and 3D animation.

Seneca's degrees, graduate certificates and diplomas are renowned for their quality and are respected by employers around the world. Our programmes promote collaborative, hands-on learning in real-world scenarios. Many offer internationally recognised professional designations that will prepare you for the working world.

You'll learn from experienced, industry-connected professors who are active in their fields. Their ongoing professional engagement ensures that your programme's curriculum stays up to date and relevant.

Many Seneca programmes have co-op components, which let you gain real-world work experience while you're in school. We're proud to maintain relationships with a range of organisations in Toronto and across Canada. These relationships improve opportunities for you to engage with the professional community and start your career once you graduate. Over 90% of employers indicate that they're pleased with the Seneca graduates they hire. This means you'll start your career with a built-in reputation for excellence.

Seneca also maintains relationships with universities in Canada and abroad. These partnerships give you the flexibility to upgrade and expand your academic credentials. For example, the University of Toronto recently announced a unique partnership that allows Seneca students to earn a diploma and a degree at both institutions in just four years.

Put simply, Seneca means success. Whether you choose to return home after graduation or stay in Toronto, studying at Seneca means a respected, high-level education that will bring your career to life.

Case study

David Jackson (Huddersfield, West Yorkshire) Fire Protection Engineering
Technology Diploma Program

'After earning my bachelor's degree I chose to study Fire Protection
Engineering Technology at Seneca College in Toronto. Seneca's
reputation in the industry, along with Toronto's global profile, made this
an easy decision. The Canadian college experience emphasises practical
instruction. My instructors are alumni with industry experience who
understand the skills necessary to gain employment after graduation.

'During my first summer I completed a work placement in my field. I
received help finding contacts in the fire protection industry, and advice
on my resume and applying for the correct visas. I worked at a school
board north of Toronto where I tested and maintained fire alarm and
suppression systems. The experience gave me insight into my field and
the opportunity to experience Canadian life outside of Toronto.

'I also lived in Seneca's halls of residence. The international student floor
created a community environment that made me feel at home. I worked
as a Resident Adviser, where I organised community events, performed
security duties and helped students with any issues and problems. In year
two I moved downtown to experience life in the city. Toronto is a vibrant,
multicultural place; the number of British people living here surprised me.
The city is a collection of distinctive neighbourhoods, including Little Italy
and Greektown, and the transit system makes it easy to get around.

'So far I'm pleased with my Canadian college experience. I have one year
left at Seneca and hope to remain in Toronto after graduation. Seneca is
giving me the tools and the confidence I need to begin a successful career.
Once I graduate I'll have a well-respected credential that will help me find
a job. I can't wait to get started.'

Algoma University

Algoma University is a thriving undergraduate university located in the scenic, lively city of Sault Ste. Marie, Ontario, at the heart of the Great Lakes along the Canada–US border.

At Algoma, you will never be in a class of more than 65 students, even in first year! Algoma University offers over 30 undergraduate degree programme options and emphasises a balance of teaching and research priorities to optimise interaction between faculty and students. In addition to the 17:1 student-to-faculty ratio, students benefit from undergraduate research opportunities, student advocacy groups, opportunities for co-operative education, a recreation centre, multiple student housing options and international exchange programs. Students enjoy all of this while being a part of a learning community that provides every student with an opportunity to be a leader and to experience success.

With its growth in recent years, the university has embraced capital expansion, including a new student residence, student centre, a new Information Communication and Technology Centre and a brand new Biosciences and Technology Convergence Centre which opened in September 2011. The Downtown Student Centre, opened in the fall of 2010, includes an upper-year residence and the University Medical Clinic.

For more information on attending Algoma University, contact: international@algomau.ca, or call 705-949-2301 ext. 4238, or visit us online at experience.algomau.ca

Case study

Oleksandr Rud (Odessa, Ukraine) Computer Science

For Oleksandr Rud, the decision to leave Odessa, in the Ukraine, to travel to Canada and study Computer Science at Algoma University was an easy one. 'I wanted a degree that would be recognised around the world,' he says, 'and a Canadian degree is an investment that will pay off in the future.'

At 31 years old with a Master's in Business Economics, Rud is not your typical undergraduate. He admits that choosing a university in Canada was a difficult task. In the end Algoma University rose to the top of his list; a decision he has 'not regretted for a minute.'

He got the impression that he would be more than just a number at Algoma University. 'Algoma is a small university where teachers pay more attention to students,' he says. 'I considered several universities, but when I contacted Algoma, I knew that it was the right place for me.'

Rud admitted being surprised by the size of Sault Ste. Marie, but he really loves that no matter where he goes he sees friendly faces and people he knows. 'Everything is so close here,' he says. 'And there are no traffic jams.' He enjoys the natural surroundings, and is looking forward to hitting the slopes at Searchmont, one of the best ski destinations in Ontario. He also enjoys travelling around Ontario, and got the chance to see Niagara Falls last summer.

In the future, Rud is hoping to remain in Canada and get some experience working for a company that develops accounting software – the perfect union of his two areas of expertise. He would like to make Canada his permanent home. 'It is beautiful here, people are very friendly, and there is a good standard of living. I'm very happy to be studying here.'

Chapter 8
Studying in Australia

What makes UK students choose to travel halfway around the world to experience study in Australia? Perhaps it's down to the combination of good-quality education, great lifestyle and reasonable entry requirements.

The education system

A significant difference between the UK and Australia is the academic year; in Australia, this runs from February to November. Universities tend to run a two-semester year with semester one running from February to June and semester two from July to November. It is possible to start most courses in July, although some courses, including medicine and dentistry, are only available to start in February. The long summer holiday runs from December to February.

University study

The style of teaching tends to be slightly different from the UK, focused on practical learning to encourage independent thought and discussion. You will need to share your views on subjects and may even be assessed on your class participation. In fact, you will probably be assessed in a range of different ways, in recognition of the fact that individual students learn in different ways.

Independent study and the development of critical thinking are encouraged, much like in the UK. You might find that you have more contact hours and a closer link with the lecturers than you would generally get in the UK.

Nearly all of Australia's universities are public, with only a few private universities. Undergraduate and postgraduate study can be offered at both pass and honours level.

> ❝ I found the facilities more modern than the UK, especially when it came to labs. I do a science so I spent plenty of time there. Teaching is great, where lectures are recorded and made available for students. This makes things so much easier, especially if you are unwell. I would say the content was interesting too, I got to learn more about Australian biology. ❞
>
> *Angela Minvalla, RMIT University*
> *(exchange student), Australia*

How to find a course

You could start your search with the official Australian government site, www.studyinaustralia.gov.au. Use the handy study wizard to research courses or institutions, check entry requirements and create a shortlist. Study in Australia also includes a mini-site for students from the UK at www.study-in-australia.org/uk.

Accreditation and quality

It is fairly straightforward to ensure that you will be studying with an approved provider. The institutions that are approved to offer degrees and other higher education qualifications can be found on the AQF Register at www.aqf.edu.au/RegisterAccreditation/AQFRegister/tabid/174/Default.aspx.

Australia also has an act in place to ensure that institutions taking on international students support them adequately; this might include helping students adjust to life in Australia as well as helping them to meet their learning goals. Go to http://cricos. deewr.gov.au to discover the list of institutions that meet these requirements.

> " I find it seems to be more personal than at UK universities. Our class is quite large, but somehow you still manage to feel a personal connection with the lecturers; they really try to get to know you and give you great feedback on assignments and how you're going throughout the year. "
>
> *Kadie O'Byrne, Murdoch University, Australia*

Academic recognition

If your institution takes lots of international students, they may understand your UK qualifications and accept you without the need to compare their standard to those offered in Australia. If the qualification is not known to them, they may ask you to have your qualifications assessed. There is no need to get an assessment done until your institution tells you to; you will have to pay for the service and it might not be needed. If required, they will put you in touch with AEI NOOSR (Australian Educational International, National Office of Overseas Skills Recognition), see www.aei.gov.au/Services-And-Resources/Pages/AEINOOSR.aspx.

Undergraduate study

Undergraduate study tends to take three to four years in Australia, with a strong emphasis on coursework. Certain courses, like medicine, can take as long as six years. Unlike

the UK, ordinary or pass degrees are the norm, generally
taking three years. Access to an honours degree is reserved for
those who have achieved particularly well. A bachelor's degree
(honours) would normally take at least four years and requires
independent research and the completion of a thesis.

The system allows for more flexibility than you get in much
of the UK. You choose a major and study a fixed number of
relevant courses, but you will also have the chance to study a
range of elective courses in different subjects. You might start
off majoring in one subject and end up graduating with a major
in a different subject, based on your interests and abilities as you
proceed through your studies.

A degree with honours is achieved after completing an
ordinary bachelor's degree with high achievement. It is
different from an honours degree.

Vocational education

TAFE (Technical and Further Education) and VET (Vocational
Education and Training) colleges may also offer some higher
education courses. They tend to offer more vocational courses
that prepare you for an industry or trade. Vocational higher
education qualifications include associate degrees and AQF
(Australian Qualifications Framework) advanced diplomas, both
of which are similar in level to HNDs or foundation degrees in
the UK.

Entry requirements

If you have passed three A levels or equivalent study, then you
should meet the general entry requirements for degree-level
study in Australia. Certain university courses require particular

grades and specific subjects to have been studied previously, while some courses will require a selection test or audition. On the whole, grade requirements tend to be slightly lower than in the UK. Programmes like medicine and dentistry are competitive, requiring high-achieving applicants with some relevant experience. Associate degrees or advanced diplomas may have lower entry requirements, although they may require specific experience or relevant previous study.

> **❝❝** The grading process is different. Instead of getting a first, 2:1, 2:2, you are awarded high distinction, distinction, credit or pass on each of your assignments, exams or units. **❞❞**
> *Vicky Otterburn, Murdoch University, Australia*

Postgraduate study

A range of different graduate qualifications are available, including graduate certificates and diplomas, master's degrees and doctorates.

- Graduate certificates (one semester) and diplomas (two semesters) are the shortest postgraduate options. They are of a similar level to postgraduate certificates and diplomas in the UK and can be used as a bridge to the study of a new subject at postgraduate level.
- A master's degree by coursework (or taught master's) tends to take two years. It may include a minor thesis.
- A master's degree by research generally takes one year after a bachelor's (honours) degree, or two years after an ordinary or pass degree.
- Doctor of Philosophy (PhD) takes from three years.

The length of your postgraduate study depends on your academic background and the subject you choose to study.

Entry requirements

The successful completion of an undergraduate degree is the standard entry requirement for postgraduate study in Australia. For some courses, you may also be required to demonstrate relevant work experience or previous research.

Entry requirements vary between institutions and their departments. The institution will be able to tell you more or you can browse institutions using the study wizard at www. studyinaustralia.gov.au.

Applying

There are some centralised admissions services in Australia. For example, the Universities Admissions Centre (UAC) administers applications for a number of institutions in New South Wales and Australian Capital Territory; the service covers undergraduate and some postgraduate courses for Australian and international students. However, in most cases, international offices require direct applications.

You need to apply to university in good time to give yourself a chance to get a visa. Final closing dates might only be a couple of months before the start of the semester, but this isn't going to give you the time to sort out all the other aspects of a move overseas. Certain courses like medicine and dentistry require a much earlier application; likewise, if you're applying for a scholarship alongside, you may need to start the process much earlier. Ideally, you should be preparing for your application a good year ahead.

The application form

Contact your chosen institution requesting information about the application process and an application form. Application forms can often be completed online. If paper-based, the application might be sent directly to the institution. Alternatively, you may choose to deal with an agent or local UK representative, depending on the requirements of the university or college.

The application process is more straightforward than the UK system. When applying direct to an institution, you will choose a first preference for your course, along with second and third options. The institution may charge you a fee to apply, ranging from around A$50 to A$100 (£31 to £62). Certain fees may be waived when applying online or through some educational agents. The UAC application allows up to six choices, with a processing fee of A$64 (£40).

Other documents

Alongside the application, you will be asked to provide an academic transcript with details of any qualifications gained, as well as details of units and unit grades. Proof of existing qualifications will be needed. If you are applying before your qualifications have been completed, you are likely to receive a conditional offer and will have to provide proof of qualifications once the results come out.

Some courses, but not all, require a personal statement and an accompanying academic reference.

Admissions tests

In some cases, an admissions test will be required for certain courses at certain institutions. Your institution will tell you more.

If a test is required, please make sure you are prepared. Although you may not be able to revise, preparing yourself for the style and time constraints of the test can make a big difference.

Undergraduate admissions tests

Applicants to medicine, dentistry and health science courses at certain universities may be required to sit either the UMAT (Undergraduate Medicine and Health Sciences Admission Test, http://umat.acer.edu.au) or the ISAT (International Student Admissions Test, http://isat.acer.edu.au). Both are available in the UK.

Applicants who haven't completed the traditional school leavers' qualifications may be asked to take the Special Tertiary Admissions Test (STAT, www.acer.edu.au/tests/stat) to assess their skills.

Postgraduate admissions tests

Postgraduate tests used in Australia include:

- the Law School Admissions Test (LSAT), http://lsat.org
- the Graduate Australian Medical Schools Admissions Test (GAMSAT), www.gamsat.acer.edu.au

> If an interview is required as part of the admissions process, you may be interviewed online or over the phone.

What next?

If your application is successful, you will receive an offer letter. Once the offer is accepted and the required tuition fees are paid (generally the fees for one semester), you will be sent an **electronic confirmation of enrolment (eCoE)**. You will need this document to apply for a visa.

Visas

In order to apply for a student visa you will need your eCoE and
the ability to financially support yourself throughout the course;
this includes the cost of tuition fees, return airfare and A$18,000
(£11,320) living costs. It is important to note that this is the
minimum required for the visa; you may need more money than
this to live on.

A further condition is adequate health insurance whilst you are in
Australia. You will also need to meet certain health requirements
and may be required to show evidence of your good character.

> A UK citizen applying for higher education in Australia
> would be classed as assessment level 1.

Contact the Australian High Commission in London (www.
uk.embassy.gov.au) for the latest applications, procedures and fees
information. You should be able to apply online and fees are £385
(as of July 2011). You shouldn't apply more than four months
in advance and should normally expect your application to be
processed within four weeks. Ask your institution if you need
further support; they are likely to have experience in this process.

Changes have been proposed in order to make Australia's
international education more competitive, including changes
to financial requirements. Further information can be found at
www.immi.gov.au and on page 211.

Costs and help with finances

The cheapest Australian undergraduate degrees may be
comparable in cost to those in England, while the most expensive

courses far exceed English fees. Scottish, Welsh and Northern Irish students will pay more in Australia than at home. So Australia is not a cheap option, but it does have some great benefits in terms of quality of education, lifestyle and opportunities.

Costs

Fee vary between different universities. According to www. studyinaustralia.gov.au, you can expect to pay annual tuition fees as follows:

- bachelor's degree – A$14,000 to A$35,000 (£8,805 to £22,012)
- master's and doctoral degree – A$15,000 to A$36,000 (£9,433 to £22,641).

Lab-based courses and those requiring specialist equipment are likely to be at the higher end of the fees scale, with courses in arts or business towards the lower end. Remember to consider the cost of books, materials and field trips too.

All students in Australia pay a student service fee of up to A$263/£165 (from February 2012) for campus services and student societies.

The strong Australian dollar means that the cost of living in Australia is currently higher than in the UK, although it also means that earnings are higher too. Australia is currently listed at number five out of 83 countries on a cost of living ranking for 2011 at www.numbeo.com.

It is a requirement of the visa that you have adequate health insurance; the cost of overseas student health cover (OSHC) starts

at a few hundred pounds per year. Visit www.studyinaustralia.
gov.au/en/Study-Costs/OSHC/
Overseas-student-health-cover for more details.

> 66 I would say clothes are cheaper here, but eating
> out and food shopping is more than one would
> expect in the UK. At first I was working with the pound
> still, converting everything to see how much it would be in
> pounds and if that was too much. But once you start
> earning the dollar it becomes relative and I stopped
> converting. 99
>
> *Kadie O'Byrne, Jersey*

The following average costs are provided by www.
studyinaustralia.gov.au:

- loaf of bread – A\$2.50 to A\$3.00 (£1.57 to £1.88)
- two litres of milk – A\$2.20 to A\$2.90 (£1.38 to £1.82)
- newspaper – A\$1.50 to A\$3.00 (94p to £1.88).

To find out about finances and budgeting in Australia, go to
www.moneysmart.gov.au/managing-my-money.

Help with finances

If you're hoping for a scholarship to help fund your studies in
Australia, you need to start early and get ready to prove yourself,
as competition is fierce. Scholarships are hard to come by and
often don't cover all the costs, so think about how you will
support yourself.

You can make a start by using the scholarships database on www. studyinaustralia.gov.au. You should talk to your university about any scholarships that they offer.

You could also take a look at the following websites:

* www.acu.ac.uk/study_in_the_commonwealth/study
* www.australiaawards.gov.au
* www.britain-australia.org.uk/affiliations/northcotetrust. html

Cultural differences

You will soon discover how multicultural Australia is; with 23% of its population born overseas, you are sure to come across other British people. Adjusting to Australia includes adjusting to its extremes of weather and its vast size. Find out about the climate in the different states and territories when you are deciding where to study.

> **"** Lifestyle and culture are different from the UK; they have an alternative way of living, from music to socialising to dressing. It is great in the sense that they appreciate their uniqueness and dress how they want. The culture is so rich and diverse where there are so many people from all walks of life. Melbourne is a huge city and is filled with so many international workers and students plus Australians, which makes it an amazing city to live in. **"**
>
> *Angela Minvalla, RMIT University, Australia*

The way of life in Australia is a bit different too; things are generally more informal and the good weather means that there is more time to enjoy life outdoors.

> **❝** The Australian lifestyle is great!!!! Everyone is so friendly, welcoming and laid back. Be expected to be referred to as a pom and people to be obsessed about your accent. You have to get up to speed with Aussie slang and lingo quite quickly, like thongs are not an underwear garment but a pair of rubber flip flops for your feet.
>
> Sport is a big part of the Aussie lifestyle; there are heaps of regular sports clubs and great facilities to use all year around. In the summer, people have BBQs regularly; you don't rush around because of the heat and spend a lot of time at the beach or around a pool with friends. There are lots of music festivals and events on offer. Australia Day is 26 January; it is a public holiday and a great day of celebration. The AFL (Australian Football League, also known as Aussie Rules) Grand Final is always a big event, whichever teams end up in it. **❞**
>
> *Vicky Otterburn, Murdoch University, Australia*

Working while studying

The opportunity to start working as soon as you start your studies is a definite benefit of study in Australia. For new students gaining a student visa, there is no need to apply for extra permission to work 20 hours per week in term time. You are permitted to work unlimited hours during holiday periods. There are a range of opportunities in pubs, bars, restaurants and shops, but you will need to balance your study and your work. You can expect wages of between A$6 and A$15 (£3.84 to £9.43) per hour.

You will need a Tax File Number (TFN) from the Australian Tax Office (www.ato.gov.au) to work and to open a bank account.

The Australian Government Department of Immigration and Citizenship (www.immi.gov.au) has the most up-to-date and detailed information.

Staying on after study

Australia is keen to welcome international students and is looking into making some changes to make it even more attractive. A post-study work option is proposed where international students with a bachelor's degree from an Australian university would have the right to work for two years in Australia in any type of job. Up to four years' post-study work could be the right of those with higher-level qualifications.

For those considering staying on a more permanent basis, Australia has a skilled migration programme targeting those who can contribute to the economy. The requirements and occupations needed vary, so choosing a course of study because it is on the skilled occupation list is not a guarantee of success; the list may well have changed by the time your course is completed. For further details, see the Department of Immigration and Citizenship website at www.immi.gov.au/skilled/general-skilled-migration.

> **❝** There are many ways to stay after you have finished studying: applying for residency, applying for a work visa or a sponsorship by a company based on an employment opportunity. The studying is the easy part, finding the job is much harder, so many more people are going to university these days and it is much more competitive for places in the workforce. **❞**
>
> *Vicky Otterburn, Murdoch*
> *University, Australia*

Pros and cons

Pros

- Strong reputation for higher education.
- Reasonable entry requirements.
- No need to apply for a work permit for up to 20 hours per week.
- Good pay for part-time work.
- Possibility of emigrating if you have the right skills.

Cons

- High cost of fees.
- High living costs (while the A$ is strong and the GB£ is weak).

Chapter 9
Studying in New Zealand

New Zealand might seem like a long way to go for an education, but many international students choose the country for its safety, quality of life and the option to settle after studies. New Zealand is a little larger in area than the UK, but with a population of only 4.5 million.

The education system

Much like Australia, New Zealand's academic year runs from late February and ends in November. The academic year incorporates two semesters, each lasting 12 weeks. You can expect breaks mid-semester and at the end of semester one, with a longer summer break after semester two (from November to February). It may be possible to join certain courses in semester two or as part of a summer school starting in January.

At all levels, students in New Zealand are encouraged to develop independent thought and defend their ideas in discussion and debate. Most taught courses are assessed by means of exams and classroom activities, which could include essays, assignments, presentations, projects and practical work. Make sure you get involved in class activities; your participation may be assessed here too.

All eight of New Zealand's universities are publicly funded. There are also a range of other institutions with degree-awarding powers: polytechnics, colleges of education and **wānanga**.

- Polytechnics or institutes of technology originally specialised in technical or vocational studies, but now offer a range of subjects and research activities.
- Colleges of education, for the most part, offer studies in the fields of early years, primary and secondary education.
- *Wānanga* provide mainly vocational educational opportunities that include Māori tradition and culture.

There are also private training establishments offering degree level education.

How to find a course

Take a look at New Zealand Educated (www.newzealandeducated.com) to search for programmes at universities, institutes of technology and polytechnics. The site also features a scholarships search option, as well as useful information about study and life in New Zealand.

Accreditation and quality

New Zealand has strong quality systems for education. In order to verify that your course or provider is accredited, you can search for approved qualifications and recognised institutions at the New Zealand Qualifications Authority website (www.nzqa.govt.nz/search). Private training establishments (PTEs) have to be registered in order to be included on this list.

Six universities in New Zealand can be found in the 2011/2012 Times Higher Education World University Rankings Top 400.

As an international student so far from home, you need to know that you will be well supported. The New Zealand Ministry of Education has a code of practice that all institutions accepting international students must adhere to. The code requires clarity and accuracy in the information you receive before you apply; ensures that international students have access to welfare support and information on life in New Zealand; and explains grievance procedures, should things go wrong. It should help you to make an informed choice on where to apply and give you a realistic idea of the support you can expect once you arrive. For more details, go to www.nzqa.govt.nz/search/.

Undergraduate study

Bachelor's degrees in New Zealand tend to take three years to complete, although some subjects take longer, up to six years for a Bachelor of Medicine. Students must successfully complete each year before moving on to the next. High achievers may opt for an additional year of study to gain an honours degree, or choose a course of at least four years with honours already incorporated.

You can often be flexible in the direction your academic studies take you, having the opportunity to try out a range of subjects. It is not unusual for the major subject you choose when you apply to end up being different from the major subject you graduate in. Your university will guide you through the process of choosing the right core and elective subjects to achieve a major in your desired subject.

Stage 1 or 100-level courses are taken in the first year, stage 2 or 200-level courses in the second year and stage 3 or 300-level courses in the third year.

It is possible to transfer credit and move between different institutions at tertiary level.

Vocational education

Qualifications in technical and vocational education are available at polytechnics, institutes of technology or in the workplace; some opportunities are available through universities and *wānanga*. Level 6 national diplomas could be compared to qualifications like HNDs or foundation degrees in the UK. If you decide to move from a national diploma to a relevant degree, it may be possible to transfer credit or to gain exemptions from the initial stages of the degree programme.

Entry requirements

Entry requirements in New Zealand tend to be lower than in the UK, as the smaller population means less of a demand for places. The grades required tend to reflect the academic level you will need to cope with the demands of the course. In most cases, you will need to have gained three A levels, or equivalent; some universities ask for three Cs at A level and there are additional grade requirements for certain courses.

At the University of Auckland, New Zealand's highest-ranking university, students need to achieve a minimum of CCC at A level to be considered for entry in 2012. There are additional course-specific requirements, for example, a minimum of CCC for Bachelor Education (Teaching), BBC for Bachelor Architectural Studies, BCC Bachelor Business and Information Management. They are not currently accepting international applicants to Bachelor Pharmacy, or for direct entry to Bachelor Medicine. If you are applying with alternatives to A levels, contact the university's international office via www.auckland.ac.nz/uoa/is-contact-auckland-international.

Postgraduate study

At postgraduate level, you might choose to study for a:

- postgraduate certificate
- postgraduate diploma
- master's degree
- doctoral degree.

All of these are of a comparable level to the same qualifications in the UK. Postgraduate certificates take one semester to complete, with postgraduate diplomas taking one year. Master's degrees tend to take two years (or less, if you have achieved an honours degree) and can be based on the completion of a thesis or have more of a focus on coursework. Doctorates would normally take three years to complete.

> If you are not ready for postgraduate study, perhaps because of your achievements at undergraduate level or maybe because you are changing subject, you could consider a graduate diploma.

Entry requirements

An undergraduate degree from a recognised institution is required to undertake postgraduate study in New Zealand. You generally need a master's degree to join a doctoral degree, although applicants with a bachelor's (honours) degree with a first or upper second classification may also be considered.

Distance learning

New Zealand has a range of distance learning providers offering education at degree level, including the Open Polytechnic of New Zealand (www.openpolytechnic.ac.nz) and Massey University (www.massey.ac.nz/massey/learning/distance-learning). Most tertiary institutions offer blended learning, delivering their education in a range of different ways (including online) to meet their students' needs.

Applying

Institutions in New Zealand require direct application, so the first step should be to contact the international office at the universities where you would like to study. They will provide all the information you need on how to apply and show you how to access the relevant application forms. They may charge an application fee. Some students choose to use the services of an agent, rather than dealing directly with the institutions.

Ideally, you should start the research process more than a year in advance, to allow time to apply for scholarships, apply for a visa and make the arrangements to move. You should plan to make contact with the universities at least six to eight months beforehand. Closing dates for applications to start in semester one (February) normally fall between September and December; to join programmes in semester two (July), you should apply by April or May. Restricted entry or competitive courses often have an earlier closing date and some may only have a February intake.

The application form

The application forms tend to be a lot shorter and simpler than the UCAS form in the UK. You will need to provide personal details, information on your previous and current academic studies and your career plans. You will be asked for a first and second choice of degree, along with details of your intended major(s).

Applications are paper-based or online. If they are online, you will still need to allow time for certified or witnessed documents to be posted or couriered to New Zealand.

Other requirements

Other documents required include academic transcripts (with details of education and qualifications) and certificates. Academic references and written statements may be requested, along with portfolios and other evidence for certain courses. The institution will also ask for a copy of your passport. Copied documents often need to be certified or witnessed by someone in the legal profession or another position of responsibility.

In addition, postgraduate applicants may need to provide two references and a CV, and may be asked to submit a research proposal.

In some cases, an interview over the phone or online may be necessary for undergraduate and postgraduate applicants.

Academic recognition

If your qualifications are unfamiliar to the international office, you may need to pay for an International Qualifications Assessment through the New Zealand Qualifications Authority: www.nzqa.govt.nz/qualifications-standards/international-qualifications/apply-for-an-international-qualifications-assessment.

What next?

If your application is successful, you will receive an offer of admission. The next step will be to apply for a visa.

Visas

Once you have accepted an offer of admission and paid your tuition fees (or the appropriate deposit), you can start to apply for a student visa. You are also likely to have to provide a chest X-ray, police certificates and accommodation details, along with evidence of funds for living costs and airfare. For courses of over nine months, you will need access to NZ$10,000/£4,784 (October 2011) per year to cover your living costs alone; you may need more than this to live on.

> When you apply for a visa, if you hope to work, tick the
> boxes under 'variation of conditions' requesting permission
> to work up to 20 hours a week during the academic year
> and full-time during the Christmas and new year holidays.

For full details of how to apply, rules and regulations and the latest
fees, go to Immigration New Zealand (www.immigration.govt.
nz). Further information can be found at the New Zealand High
Commission in London (www.nzembassy.com/united-kingdom).
You should allow four to six weeks for processing. The fee is
currently £125.

Most international offices have lots of experience in helping
students through these processes. They will know the problems
that previous applicants have encountered and should support
you to make a successful application for a visa.

Once you have a visa you will need to follow certain requirements
in order to retain it, like attending your course and achieving
certain standards. Your visa will only last for a maximum of
one academic year, so you will need to reapply for subsequent
years of study. You may be able to renew it online through your
institution in subsequent years.

Costs and help with finances

New Zealand is unlikely to offer a cheaper option for education
at undergraduate level; some of the cheapest university
undergraduate fees in New Zealand are comparable in cost to the
most expensive in the UK.

At postgraduate level, the costs can be higher than in the UK,
although there is an incentive to study PhDs, making New
Zealand a very attractive proposition.

Costs

Individual tertiary institutions set their own fees, which will vary depending on the course you choose. According to New Zealand Educated (www.newzealandeducated.com), annual tuition fees for undergraduate study range from NZ$18,000 to NZ$25,000 (£8,612 to £11,961) per year. Courses at polytechnics or institutes of technology may be lower than NZ$18,000 (£8,612) per year, making them a more affordable option.

Postgraduate tuition fees for international students can be as much as NZ$40,000 (£19,138) per year. However, international PhD students pay the same fees as students from New Zealand, starting at around NZ$5,000 (£2,392) per year.

Although you will be required to prove access to NZ$10,000 (£4,784) per year for visa purposes, New Zealand Educated suggests allowing as much as double that amount for living costs. It includes some helpful indications of costs on its website www.nzeducated.com/int/en/guide/on_arrival/living_costs. In comparison to the rest of the world, New Zealand is ranked number 16 of 83 countries on a 2011 cost of living ranking at www.numbeo.com; the UK is listed just higher at number 14.

Remember to budget for medical and travel insurance; international students are legally obliged to hold this throughout their period of study in New Zealand.

Help with finances

A range of scholarships are available, although you will need to compete with other applicants. Apply early, follow all the guidelines and be prepared to supplement any scholarship with other sources of funding; most scholarships will not cover all costs. Scholarships include the Commonwealth Scholarship and Fellowship Plan and international doctoral research scholarships.

You can search for scholarships at www.newzealandeducated. com/int/en/institutions_courses/scholarships. This searches options including national and university-specific awards. Talk to your university or polytechnic about the range of scholarships they administer.

Take a look at the Association of Commonwealth Universities website, for details of their scholarships, awards and fellowships www.acu.ac.uk/study_in_the_commonwealth/study.

Cultural differences

New Zealand is a multicultural nation with an informal way of doing things. One in seven New Zealanders is Māori, so their language and culture forms an important part of the national identity. In New Zealand, you can expect an outdoor lifestyle with the opportunity to get involved with sports and a range of cultural activities.

Although there will be similarities to the UK, don't assume that life will be the same; there will be cultural differences. It is helpful to find out about the culture and way of life in New Zealand in order to prepare yourself for a successful transition. Talking to other people who have already made the transition can be helpful. There are many websites for expats that might help in this process. Your university's international office may be able to help too.

Working while studying

If you have ticked the relevant boxes on the student visa application (variation of conditions), you may be allowed to work up to 20 hours during academic term and full-time during the summer holidays. Make sure you have permission before you start working and follow the visa requirements to the letter. Your right to work can normally be found on your student visa. You can apply for a variation of conditions at a later date, if necessary.

Don't assume that you will find work immediately. It can be hard to find the right job to fit in with your studies and your visa requirements. You will also need to consider how you balance your academic studies and your working life. Take a look at Student Job Search for opportunities in your area www.sjs.co.nz. You will need an Inland Revenue Department (IRD) number too. Find out more at www.ird.govt.nz/how-to/irdnumbers.

Staying on after study

If you hope to stay on in New Zealand after finishing your studies, there are a number of schemes currently in operation. The government is keen to retain young people with the right skills and knowledge to contribute to the New Zealand economy. If you hope to emigrate, you may decide to choose your subject based on skills shortage areas at the time you apply; don't forget that these lists are subject to change and may well be different by the time you complete your studies.

If you don't have a job offer you have the following options.

- **Graduate job search visa**
  Recent graduates from tertiary institutes in New Zealand can apply for a visa of up to 12 months giving them time to search for a skilled job (and to work on a temporary basis while searching). On finding a skilled, long-term job, you can apply for a graduate work experience visa for two years.
- **Skilled migrant category visa**
  This is a points-based residence visa, with points gained for a job offer, experience, qualifications and so on.

There are a number of options if you are offered a job considered to be in a shortage area.

- **Essential skills visa**
  The essential skills visa allows those with a job offer to work in New Zealand (provided a New Zealander cannot be found to do the job).
- **Long term skills shortage list (LTSSL) visa**
  The LTSSL visa is a 30-month work visa for skills shortage areas; after two years, holders of this visa can apply for a resident visa.
- **Skilled migrant category visa**
  A job offer will enhance the points you can gain on this points-based residence visa.

For more information see www.dol.govt.nz/immigration and www.immigration.govt.nz/migrant. The information is complex and subject to change. Your university may be able to put you in touch with relevant sources of support for this process.

Pros and cons

Pros

- Range of internationally recognised qualifications.
- Support for international students.
- Reasonable entry requirements.
- Possibilities to stay on and work afterwards.

Cons

- Current costs of living.
- Far from home.

Chapter 10
The rest of the world

You might imagine that you wouldn't find students from the UK studying right across the globe; well, prepare to be surprised. Although a less common choice than Australia or the States, some UK students already opt for South Africa, the Caribbean or Singapore as their place of learning. This chapter introduces you to some of the countries you might not have considered for your studies.

Countries where English is an official language

Hong Kong

Hong Kong is a special administrative region of China, offering a cosmopolitan lifestyle and a gateway to China. As Hong Kong was under British rule for many years, English is still an official language. Street signs and announcements on public transport are in English, Cantonese and often Putonghua (Mandarin).

Now under Chinese rule, Hong Kong has its own currency and political system and a separate identity from the rest of China.

Higher education in Hong Kong

Although the education system in Hong Kong has been influenced by the UK, with three-year bachelor's degrees the norm, the introduction of a more international system means that four-year bachelor's degrees will be offered from 2012. Some joint degrees or specialist fields will take a year or two longer. Ordinary and honours degrees are available, along with associate degrees at a lower academic level. Master's degrees will take one to two years and doctorate degrees a minimum of three years to complete.

> If you are interested in opportunities in China, you will find that degrees from Hong Kong are compatible with Chinese qualifications. Beginners' courses in Cantonese and Putonghua will be available; some programmes even offer the chance of a year in Beijing or Shanghai.

The academic year runs from early September to May, with orientation activities taking place in late August. The year is split into two equal semesters. Hong Kong features 15 degree-awarding institutions made up of a combination of public and private establishments. Higher education is split between universities, polytechnics and technical institutes.

To find out more about studying in Hong Kong or to search for a course or an institution, go to Study HK (http:// studyinhongkong.edu.hk/eng).

Applying

Entry requirements vary, but satisfactory performance at A level should meet the general requirements for undergraduate level study. For example, the University of Hong Kong (currently placed above University College London and the University of Edinburgh on the Times Higher Education World University Rankings Top 200) asks for a minimum of three Es at A level (not including languages) to meet the general academic requirements. Scottish students are asked for a minimum of BCCCC in their Highers. There may be additional subject requirements and you will need to have taken a language at GCSE or equivalent level. An honours degree is required for entry to postgraduate study.

Application deadlines vary, but may be as early as December or as late as May for a September start. Applications should be made directly to your chosen university and are likely to include:

* personal statement
* reference
* predicted grades plus previous educational achievement
* research statement (for postgraduate research).

The University of Hong Kong also looks for evidence of second language ability (evidenced by a grade E or better at GCSE) and state that they 'value all-roundedness'.

Costs

According to Study HK, annual tuition fees on government-funded programmes range from HK$75,000 to $120,000 (£6,208–£9,933).

Accommodation in university halls of residence is reasonably priced, but space is at a premium in Hong Kong and private rental can be astronomical. As Study HK explains, 'If you live in University-provided residence halls or hostels, you'll pay a modest HK$5,000 to HK$20,200 (£413 to £1,655) per semester; expect to pay that much per month if living off-campus.' Most institutions prioritise accommodation for international students; some universities even guarantee it.

When weighing up living costs, Study HK estimates, 'HK$30,000–HK$60,000 (£2,483–£4,966) per year for additional costs, including food, leisure, transportation, and personal items, depending on how extravagantly you plan to live.' Hong Kong comes in at number 33 out of 83 countries on a cost of living ranking for 2011. Compare that to the UK, which is listed at a pricier number 14 (www.numbeo.com).

Scholarships are available, although opportunities are limited and most, although not all, are restricted to those displaying academic excellence. See Study HK for a list of scholarships or talk to your institution for further details.

Three of Hong Kong's 15 degree-awarding institutions can be found in the Times Higher Education World University Rankings Top 200 2011/2012.

Visas

Once you have been accepted and have found a place to live, you can then apply for a student visa. This should be arranged through the university which will normally act as your local sponsor to support the visa application. You'll need to provide proof of academic qualifications, proof of accommodation and proof of finances. There is no specific amount required by the Hong Kong Immigration Department; your university will be able to give you an idea of appropriate amounts to cover academic and living costs.

For more information on visas go to www.immd.gov.hk. The application can take up to eight weeks to be processed and will need to be renewed every year. Your institution will be able to support you through the process.

Working while studying

Although a student visa doesn't normally allow work alongside study, there may be opportunities to take internships, campus-based work or work during the holidays. Talk to your university about these procedures and whether you can apply for a 'no objection letter' allowing certain conditions of employment.

After you complete your degree, you can apply for a 12-month stay without a job offer.

Pros and cons
Pros

- High proportion of highly ranked institutions.
- A gateway to China.
- English as an official language.
- Chance to experience a different culture.
- Modern, efficient and cheap public transport.

Cons

- Private accommodation is small and expensive.
- Air pollution and humidity.
- Densely populated.

South Africa

Why South Africa? The Rainbow Nation offers diversity, culture and an outdoor lifestyle combined with a great climate and low cost of living.

Higher education in South Africa

Higher education is offered at universities, universities of technology and comprehensive universities. Traditional universities offer academic study, while universities of technology focus on practical or vocational options; comprehensive universities offer both. There are some private universities in South Africa. The languages of English and Afrikaans are both used.

Bachelor's degrees take at least three years (up to six for medicine), with an additional year of study to achieve an honours degree. A master's degree takes at least one year, while doctorates require a minimum of two years' research.

The academic year runs from February to November. Higher Education South Africa (http://hesa.org.za) has links to all the public universities, where you can browse the courses on offer.

South Africa has three universities in the 2011/2012 Times Higher Education World University Rankings Top 400.

Applying

Applications should be made directly to your chosen institution, which will often charge an application fee. They will advise you how to get a certificate of exemption to validate your international qualifications.

Two A levels plus three GCSEs (or four Scottish Highers plus one Standard Grade) should meet the general requirements for undergraduate programmes in South Africa. For further details, see the South African Matriculation Board website (www.hesa-enrol.ac.za/mb/forpres.htm). There will be additional requirements for specific subjects. A bachelor's (honours) degree should meet the general entry criteria for a master's degree.

While postgraduate research programmes may be flexible about when you can apply, you will need time to apply for a study permit and to prepare for the move. South African post can be slow, so you should apply as early as possible. Deadline dates for undergraduate and taught postgraduate courses vary; expect to apply at least six months before the course starts, maybe earlier if you're also applying for a scholarship.

Costs

Fees vary depending on what you study and where. For example, the University of Western Cape charges between ZAR30,000 to 40,000 (£2,252 to £3,003) per year for its courses, recommends ZAR11,000 to 16,500 (£825 to £1,238) per year for a single room, ZAR18,000 (£1,351) for food and around ZAR4,500 (£337) for books and stationery. International term fees or residence fees may also be payable. The international office will be able to tell you more about the costs at your chosen university.

> **❝❝** The cost of studying at University of Cape Town is almost identical to the UK, if not a little cheaper, even before the increase in tuition fees in the UK. **❞❞**
>
> *Will Perkins, Bachelor's student, South Africa*

> **❝❝** My tuition fees were more than in the UK as I was an international student. However, that was more than compensated for by the relatively low cost of living in Cape Town compared to London. For this reason, my overall cost of living and studying in Cape Town for a year and a half was about 50% less than it would have been had I studied in London. **❞❞**
>
> *Nick Parish, Master's student, South Africa*

In a 2011 cost of living ranking produced by www.numbeo.com, South Africa is listed at number 37 of 83 countries, much lower than the UK and much of Europe.

Visas

Once you have received a written offer, you will need to apply for a study permit at the South African High Commission (http://

southafricahouseuk.com/). There is a £35 processing fee and an expected turnaround time of 30 working days. You will need to prove that you can support yourself financially and will be asked for a medical report and a police certificate as well as proof of medical cover. The study permit will need to be renewed every year.

Further information

International Education Association of South Africa (www. studysa.co.za) has a helpful guide for international students.

Pros and cons

Pros

- Great climate.
- Low cost of living.
- Outdoor lifestyle.

Cons

- Crime rate.

Malaysia

Malaysia has hundreds of higher education institutions to choose from and strong links with the UK. Many overseas universities have chosen to base campuses there, including institutions from the UK like the University of Nottingham, Liverpool John Moores and Newcastle University (Medicine).

Other institutions offer dual degrees incorporating UK qualifications. For example, a BEng (Hons) Civil Engineering from INTI International University comes complete with an MEng from the University of Bradford, subject to certain academic conditions.

Higher education in Malaysia

The academic year in Malaysia is changing to a September start to bring it into line with the northern hemisphere; certain courses also have intakes in January or May. In Malaysia, a bachelor's degree takes three to four years to complete, with the exception of courses like medicine and dentistry, which take five years. A master's degree will take between one and three years and can be coursework-based, research-based or a combination. A minimum of two years' subsequent study can lead to a doctorate.

Courses taught in English may be restricted to private or international universities at undergraduate level. At postgraduate level, there should be English-medium options at public universities too. Only selected private institutions approved by the Ministry of Home Affairs are open to students from overseas; you will need to check that your chosen university has the appropriate permissions to recruit international students. All public universities can recruit from overseas.

Study Malaysia (www.studymalaysia.com) has a course search, along with useful information about education, costs and the country itself.

Costs

Tuition fees vary from institution to institution. Universiti Teknologi Malaysia charges undergraduate fees of around 9,500RM (£1,926) per year (which includes a range of additional fees, registration, student services and so on). Postgraduate fees range from 7,052RM to 8,452RM (£1,430 to £1,714). University of Nottingham, Malaysia has annual undergraduate fees ranging from 33,500RM (£6,795), with master's degrees from 42,000RM (£8,519) and PhDs from 33,500RM (£6,795) per year. INTI International's BEng (Hons) Civil Engineering (with dual award from University of Bradford) costs 43,500RM (£8,823) per year.

In most cases, a UK degree will have similar tuition fees whether you decide to study it in the UK or Malaysia; if you choose to study overseas, you will benefit from the lower cost of living and the international experience. Living costs are considerably lower than in the UK. Malaysia is rated number 73 out of 83 countries on a cost of living index for 2011 (www.numbeo. com). Information on funding and scholarships can be found at www.studymalaysia.com, at www.acu.ac.uk/study_in_the_commonwealth/study and from your institution.

Applying

International applicants will need to apply direct to their chosen institutions, either online or via a paper application. A personal statement will be a key component of the application. You should apply by the required deadline date and at least six months before you are due to commence your studies.

Visas

Your university will apply for a student pass on your behalf; once this is granted you will also receive a multiple entry visa. More information is available through the Malaysian High Commission in London, www.kln.gov.my/perwakilan/london.

Pros and cons

Pros

- Reasonable tuition fees for Malaysian degrees.
- Opportunity to gain degrees from USA, UK and Australia in a country with a low cost of living.
- Chance to experience a different culture.
- Tropical climate.

Cons

- No world-renowned Malaysian universities.

- Need approval of your institution before you can work during term-time.
- Not all universities are open to international students.

Singapore

Singapore may be small, but it is a hotspot for financial services, an important trading centre in the heart of Asia and home to the world's busiest port. Its education system is well-recognised around the world and compatible in level to education in the UK. English is widely used, particularly for education and business, and most courses are taught in the language.

Higher education in Singapore

The academic year runs from the beginning of August to early May and is divided into two semesters. Bachelor's degrees are available at ordinary level (after three years' study) and with honours (after four years). Most master's degrees take one year, with a minimum of three years required to complete a PhD.

Singapore has four autonomous public universities and a publicly funded institute of technology (which provides an industry-focused university education):

- National University of Singapore
- Nanyang Technological University
- Singapore Management University
- Singapore University of Technology and Design
- Singapore Institute of Technology.

You will find one private university, SIM University, along with a number of other private institutions and international universities with a campus in Singapore.

To search for a course or find out about an institution, go to Singapore Education, http://app.singaporeedu.gov.sg. The resources section on this website has links to many other useful sites.

Contact Singapore (www.contactsingapore.sg) has a lot of information on living in Singapore.

Applying

At undergraduate level, universities will be looking for good passes in three A levels, so you should be aiming to apply with grades at C or above. In some cases, particularly if you're applying before you know your results, the universities will require the SAT or ACT admissions tests. (For more information on the SAT and ACT, see the US-UK Fulbright Commission website, www.fulbright.co.uk/study-in-the-usa/undergraduate-study/admissions-tests.)

At postgraduate level, you are likely to need 2:1 in an honours degree combined with GMAT (www.mba.com) or GRE (www.ets.org/gre) admissions tests for specific subjects. See individual universities for entry criteria and test requirements.

Applications should be made direct to the university's admissions or international office. Undergraduate applicants can select up to five potential courses. As part of the application, you might have to write a short essay on your achievements or reflect on any positions of responsibility. Postgraduate research applicants will need to write a research proposal. At both undergraduate and postgraduate level you will need to provide references.
The university will charge you an application fee of around S$50–S$75 (£25–£36). You can apply from September or October.

At the National University of Singapore, you will not be eligible for competitive courses like dentistry, law, medicine or nursing if you apply with predicted grades. If this is the case at your chosen university or with your chosen course, wait until you have your actual grades to make the application; this might mean waiting for the next intake, but can also result in exemption from certain admissions tests.

Costs

Tuition fees in Singaporean universities are high, but are subsidised by the government through the tuition grant scheme. This scheme is open to international students on the condition that you work for three years after graduation for a Singaporean company; this can be deferred for reasons including further study. You can find out more at the Ministry of Education website (www.moe.gov.sg or http://tgonline.moe.gov.sg) or from your university.

The National University of Singapore (ranked above the London School of Economics and the University of Manchester on the Times Higher Education World University Rankings Top 200 2011/2012) charges fees for undergraduate degrees ranging from S$31,340/£15,438 to S$124,280/£61,221(for medicine and dentistry). These fees fall to between S$12,340 and S$35,280 (£6,078 and £17,379) when the tuition grant is included.

At postgraduate level, Singapore Management University will charge S$24,080 (£11,862) for master's degrees and S$17,200 (£8,472) for PhDs in 2012: this includes the tuition grant. Without a tuition grant, you would be looking at fees of S$40,180/£20,000 (master's) and S$28,700/£14,137 (PhDs).

Additional fees may be payable for the students' union, exams and health services.

Scholarships are available and can be searched for on the Singapore Education website (www.singaporeedu.gov.sg), at the Ministry of Education site (see page 237) or discussed with your university.

Singapore Education (www.singaporeedu.gov.sg) estimates living costs of S$750 to S$2,000 (£369 to £985) per month. It falls at number 20 of 83 countries listed on a cost of living ranking per country (www.numbeo.com), so is considered less expensive than the UK at the moment.

Visas

You will need a student pass to study in Singapore. Your university will register you on the Immigration and Checkpoints Authority online registration system (SOLAR) and you will then need to complete an online application. There is no required amount of money that you need to provide evidence of, so you should talk to your university about an advisable amount. You won't receive the student pass until you arrive in Singapore, so you will first be granted a social visit pass at the airport.

Find out more at the Immigration and Checkpoints Authority (www.ica.gov.sg) or the High Commission for the Republic of Singapore in London (www.mfa.gov.sg/london).

Working while studying

International students can work up to 16 hours per week under certain conditions and the approval of the university or polytechnic that you are studying in. You would need to talk to your institution to request a letter of authorisation.

On graduating, you may be able to apply for an employment pass eligibility certificate (EPEC), giving you the chance to stay on in

Singapore for up to one year to look for work. This pass doesn't allow you to work, so, if you are successful in finding a job, you will then need to obtain an employment pass before you can start. For more detail see the Ministry of Manpower (www.mom.gov.sg).

Pros and cons
Pros

- Chance to experience another culture.
- Modern city-state with a high standard of living.
- Tropical climate.

Cons

- Densely populated.
- Competitive entry.
- Need approval of your university before you can work in term-time.

The Caribbean

A number of UK students head off to the Caribbean for their studies, particularly for medical or dental programmes, with over 60 medical schools listed there. Many opt for international universities with a base in the Caribbean that prepare students for a medical or dental career in countries like the USA, Canada or the UK. This list might include St George's University Grenada, Ross University, the American University of the Caribbean and Saba University School of Medicine. St George's recruits from the UK and prepares students for medical practice in a number of countries, including the UK, whereas the other institutions tend to have more of a North American focus.

St George's University has around 60 UK students, mainly in the School of Medicine. Within the School of Medicine, the pass rates are currently over 96%, although the fees are very high. The entire medical programme (including accommodation) could cost in the region of US$215,000 (£138,709). The university has intakes in August and January and you should apply direct.

There are also local universities offering courses, most notably the University of the West Indies (UWI), a regional university representing 15 countries with four sites across the Caribbean. Its fees at undergraduate level are around US$13,000 (£8,387) per year, with the exception of medicine, which is around US$23,000 (£14,838).

Make sure you check the validity of any professional qualification with the relevant professional body. If you intend to practise medicine in the UK, you should check requirements with the General Medical Council. For a list of the relevant professional bodies in the UK, see the website of the National Contact Point for Professional Qualifications in the UK at www.ukncp.org.uk.

Unfortunately, there isn't one source of information to find other recognised universities. You could use the high commission websites in the UK; for example, the Jamaica High Commission in the UK at www.jhcuk.org/citizens/universities lists UWI, University of Technology and Northern Caribbean University. You could also use accreditation organisations like the University Council of Jamaica, the Barbados Accreditation Council and the Accreditation Council of Trinidad and Tobago. Find contact details for these and other accreditation bodies at CANQATE (Caribbean Area Network for Quality Assurance in Tertiary Education), www.canqate.org/Links/RelatedLinks.aspx. Once you are sure that your university is recognised and accredited, you can go to their website for the latest information on courses, fees and how to apply.

Pros and cons
Pros

- Tropical climate.
- Low cost of living.
- Chance to gain medical training relevant to more than one country.

Cons

- A range of education systems on offer with no single reliable source of information.
- High costs for medical and dental studies.

Countries where English isn't widely used

Across the rest of the world there are options for those wanting to study in English. Even in places where English is not widely spoken you will find pockets of opportunity for UK students. We will explore a few of those countries here.

China
The Chinese government is investing heavily in its higher education and is keen to attract international students. The growth of China as an economic force means that awareness of Chinese culture and language is likely to be an important asset.

How to find a course
You can search for degree programmes on the CUCAS (China's University and College Admission System) website, www. cucas.edu.cn. Once your search brings up a list of courses, you

can select those taught in English. The Chinese Ministry of Education also holds a list of English-taught programmes in Chinese higher education, as well as information on scholarships; visit www.moe.edu.cn/publicfiles/business/htmlfiles/moe/moe_2812/200906/48835.html.

There are age restrictions for international students hoping to study higher education in China.

- Undergraduate applicants should be under 25.
- Master's degree applicants should be under 35.
- Doctoral applicants should be under 40.

Higher education in China

The academic year runs from September to mid-July and international students should apply between February and April.

Bachelor's degrees normally take four years to complete, master's degrees take two to three years and doctorates take from three years; all are similar in level to those offered in the UK.

Traditionally, the style of teaching in China has been more teacher-centred than in the UK. You may find that this is less of an issue on English-taught courses aimed at international students.

Applying

A level study is generally required for undergraduate courses, with a bachelor's degree (plus two references) required for master's study, and a master's degree (plus two references) for doctoral study.

Applications can be made direct to universities or online through CUCAS. If applying through CUCAS, additional documentation (copy of passport, academic transcripts and police certificates, for example) can be scanned or clearly photographed. CUCAS charges a service fee of US$50 (£32) for up to six applications, with applications processed within two to four weeks. Institutions also charge an application fee before they will issue the school admission notice required for a visa; they will normally take a further four to eight weeks to process an application.

Visas

For study in China of over six months, you will need an X-visa. You can apply through the Chinese Embassy. Go to www. visaforchina.org for more details.

Costs

CUCAS advises of tuition fees around US$2,000–US$5,000 (£1,290–£3,225) per year and living expenses of around US$5,000 (£3,335), although other organisations seem to suggest more money will be needed. China is listed as number 75 (of 83) on the Numbeo cost of living ranking by country 2011; it is the lowest-ranked country for cost of living featured in this book.

Full and partial scholarships are available through the China Scholarship Council (www.csc.edu.cn). If you are proficient in a Chinese language, you may be eligible for a Chinese Government Scholarship. Search for scholarships on the Ministry of Education website (www.moe.edu.cn) and through CUCAS (www.cucas.edu.cn).

Pros and cons
Pros

- An increasingly powerful world economic force.
- Investment in higher education.
- Chance to experience a new culture.

Cons

- Language barrier outside the classroom.
- A new setting for international students.
- Issues around censorship and political restrictions.
- Age restrictions for study.

Saudi Arabia

Although most courses are in Arabic, there are opportunities in English at certain Saudi universities. For example, Saudi Arabia's first international university, King Abdullah University of Science and Technology (www.kaust.edu.sa), opened in 2009 and offers postgraduate courses taught in English.

Higher education in Saudi Arabia

Public and private universities in Saudi Arabia are overseen by the Ministry for Higher Education. Bachelor's degrees run for a minimum of four years, master's degrees take two years and doctorates from three years. Qualifications are of a similar level to the UK. For a list of universities go to the Ministry of Higher Education website at www.mohe.gov.sa (click the letter E in the top left for an English version). Some institutions are not open to women.

Life in Saudi Arabia

Saudi Arabia is a Muslim country where Islamic law is strictly enforced. Life differs greatly from the UK; mixed gatherings are not customary and alcohol is not permitted. Recreation activities for men centre on sport, with many activities for women restricted.

Applying

Applications should be made direct to your chosen university.

Costs

Tuition fees vary, with individual universities setting their own. Scholarships and fellowships are available; talk to your chosen university about what is available.

Saudi Arabia is listed at number 23 (out of 83) on the Numbeo cost of living ranking for 2011 (www.numbeo.com). The UK is at number 14.

Visas

Once you have been offered a place, you should then start the process of applying for a visa or entry permit. For details, go to the Ministry of Foreign Affairs website at www.mofa.gov.sa or www.saudiembassy.org.uk.

Alternatives

Qatar's Education City is a huge complex of education and research facilities and includes universities from the USA, France and the UK. Find out more at the Qatar Foundation for Education, Science and Community Development at www.qf.org. qa/education/universities.

Pros and cons

Pros

- Investment in higher education.
- Chance to experience a new culture.

Cons

- Saudi universities (and Middle Eastern universities in general) are not well-represented on the world university rankings.
- Social and recreational activities may be restricted, particularly for women.

Japan

Japan has some international students, but they tend to come from other Eastern Asian countries like China, the Republic of Korea and Taiwan. The government is seeking to attract more international students; they have chosen to invest in higher education and are also extending the study options available in English.

A group of universities known as Global 30 has been set up to boost the number of international students in Japan. They receive extra funding and are developing an increasing number of degrees taught in English.

- Doshisha University
- Keio University
- Kyoto University
- Kyushu University
- Meiji University
- Nagoya University
- Osaka University
- Ritsumeikan University
- Sophia University
- Tohoku University
- University of Tokyo
- University of Tsukuba
- Waseda University.

Find out more, including links to all these universities at Japanese Universities for Motivated People (JUMP), visit www.uni.international.mext.go.jp/global30.

Higher education in Japan

Currently, most institutions in Japan require proficiency in Japanese, but there are some exceptions. A number of Japanese universities offer master's and doctoral degrees in English, although the options are more limited at undergraduate level. JASSO (Japan Student Services Organisation) has a list of university degree courses offered in English, see www.jasso.go.jp.

There are far more private than public universities. Japan has some international universities and overseas universities with campuses in Japan.

The academic year starts in April and is run as a two-semester system, April to September and October to March, with holidays at intervals throughout the year. It should take you four years to complete a bachelor's degree; the first two years offer more general studies, while the final two years allow you to specialise. Study at master's level tends to take two years, with a further three years required for a doctorate.

You should apply direct to your chosen university; you may be required to sit an entrance exam.

Sample courses

Doshisha University's Insitute for the Liberal Arts (http://ila. doshisha.ac.jp) offers Japanese cultural, business and political education in English. You can study a four-year undergraduate degree alongside intensive study of Japanese language. Total fees (tuition, admission and facilities fees) are JPY1109,000 (£9,247) for the 2012 academic year, but all international students will receive some form of discount through international scholarships. Doshisha University also offers postgraduate programmes taught in English.

The International University of Japan (www.iuj.ac.jp) is a private university offering master's degrees. It charges annual fees of JPY1,900,000 (£15,843) with a JPY300,000 (£2,500) admission fee.

It suggests minimum monthly living costs of JPY95,000 (£792), although other sources suggest substantially more will be required.

Temple University, Japan offers an American education with a Japanese location. As well as business, economics and general studies, you can also choose a major in Asian studies and Japanese language, see www.tuj.ac.jp.

> In 2010, 452 UK students were studying in Japan, with 295 UK students completing studies of less than one year (JASSO, www.jasso.go.jp).

Costs

See individual universities for costs. Education Japan (http://educationjapan.org) suggests allowing JPY600,000 to JPY1000,000 (£5,000 to £8,338) for annual tuition fees. You need to know that there are other fees payable to the university that can increase this figure somewhat. JASSO has information on scholarships, living and accommodation costs at www.jasso.go.jp.

University accommodation is substantially cheaper than private rented accommodation, so check whether your chosen university will guarantee accommodation for you. In private accommodation, in addition to rent, there are deposits and 'thank you' money to be paid, which can be around four months' rent (and sometimes more).

Japan had a reputation for being expensive; however, it is now ranked number 11 out of 83 countries on the cost of living rankings (www.numbeo.com); that's lower than Norway, Finland, the Netherlands and Australia.

Visas

You will need a student visa in order to study in Japan; your university will act as a sponsor for the visa process and should obtain a certificate of eligibility for you. This will need to be processed at the Embassy of Japan (www.uk.emb-japan.go.jp) in the UK (or the country where you are resident). Student visa holders need the approval of their university and the immigration office to be able to work.

For information on study in Japan, go to www.studyjapan.go.jp/en.

Pros and cons

Pros

- A culture which combines tradition and cutting-edge technology.
- Drive to increase numbers of international students.

Cons

- Language barrier outside the classroom.
- Relatively few western students at present.
- The need to factor in additional fees for study and accommodation.

Hopefully, the information about these countries will have whetted your appetite and given you a starting point for your research. Of course, the countries profiled here are not the only options open to you; many other countries are keen to attract students from the UK. If you are interested in studying elsewhere in the world, you can use the information in this book (see Chapters 2, 3 and 4) to help ensure that the education you opt for is the right step for you.

The University of the West Indies

Why not study at the University of the West Indies, Mona?

The University of the West Indies (UWI) is an innovative, internationally competitive, contemporary university deeply rooted in the Caribbean and committed to offering quality higher education. It is the largest tertiary level institution in the English-speaking Caribbean with campuses at Mona and Montego Bay in Jamaica, St. Augustine in Trinidad and Tobago, Cave Hill in Barbados and its Open Campus. While its programmes are international in scope, the UWI has a unique Caribbean focus. This strong emphasis on Caribbean issues makes the UWI the ideal educational institution for local and international students with an interest in Caribbean society.

Our undergraduate degree programmes are normally three years, on a two semester system, beginning in August and ending in May. Postgraduate diplomas and higher degree programmes are offered through a number of Institutes and Centres of Excellence affiliated with the University. Special group and summer programmes in Caribbean Cultural Studies are also available during the winter, spring and summer breaks.

Sports

Hone your skills or discover your talent in Track and Field, Cricket, Football, Basketball, Hockey, Rugby, Volleyball, Table Tennis, Tennis and Swimming at the Mona Bowl for Sporting Excellence, site of the UWI-Usain Bolt Regupol Track.

Entry requirements

For further information, contact our Senior Assistant Registrar (International Students), at iso@uwimona.edu.jm or visit our website www.mona.uwi.edu

Case study

Sachiyo Morimoto (Shikoku Island in Japan) Bachelor of Arts degree in African Diaspora Studies[ebold]

When Sachiyo Morimoto came to the University of the West Indies, Mona from Shikoku Island in Japan, it marked the end of a 10 year journey to fulfill her dream of studying at the institution.

Sachiyo found out about the UWI, Mona from a Japanese professor who had undertaken research at the Campus in the early 1990s. Over the next 10 years, she published several books on Jamaica, while making the necessary preparations to get to Mona.

Now pursuing the Bachelor of Arts degree programme in African Diaspora Studies, Sachiyo is convinced that she made the right decision. 'The UWI Mona is one of the best for African Diaspora Studies and I can engage in a participatory observation at the same time', she says. 'The lecturers are also very helpful, knowledgeable and skilled in teaching and our classes are well structured.'

Sachiyo is one of approximately 400 international students studying at the UWI, Mona Campus. Students from Belgium, Botswana, Burma, Canada, China, Denmark, France, Germany, Guadeloupe, Japan, Nigeria, Norway, Puerto Rico, Sweden, the United Kingdom, and the United States of America as well as from all 15 countries in the English-speaking Caribbean are enrolled at Mona. She maintains that 'even when we don't talk to each other, I feel that we share the same feeling because we are going through the same new experience at UWI Mona.'

Chapter 11
Student profiles

Now you can find out more from the students who have actually gone and studied overseas. Discover what they gained from the experience; their highs and lows; the challenges they have faced and the highlights of their time spent studying abroad.

STUDENT CASE STUDY
Clare Higgins, the Netherlands

Clare Higgins is studying for a Bachelor's degree in European Studies at The Hague University of Applied Sciences in the Netherlands.

The decision to is studying abroad was made at the last minute. 'I just missed my offer from Lancaster University and unfortunately I lost my place. I didn't want to have a gap year, because I have heard from friends that it is so much more difficult to motivate yourself to study again. I had originally thought of studying abroad last year, but finding information was difficult.

'After results day my teacher recommended that I get in touch with Mark Huntingdon from A Star Future because she knew that I would be really interested in his information on clearing places at foreign universities. The day after I contacted Mark, I went to The Hague to visit a university that offered a very attractive course. I decided to join this degree because the course was ideal and I felt that this was a fantastic opportunity.'

Being such a late applicant brought some challenges. 'The Dutch universities start earlier so I had not even enrolled, had no financial aid or plan, don't speak any Dutch and had no accommodation, so I felt very unprepared. However when I arrived, the director of studies was incredibly helpful. There are still some issues such as finance and upgrading my status that I need to sort out, as the different departments are not always sure what the procedure is.'

Although it was a concern beforehand, Clare's lack of Dutch language skills hasn't caused any issues. 'There really is no language barrier here, as all lessons and discussions are in English because it is the one common language. The classes have a large number of international students whose level of English is very impressive. You can speak English in all shops and restaurants and there is no problem being understood. However it is a great opportunity to learn the language in school and then practise it out and about.'

Clare is enjoying her academic studies in the Netherlands. 'I feel I am having a much more international experience here than I ever would have had in England. This adds value to my degree, European Studies, as I am studying in a diverse environment which is reflected in the debates and classes that we take part in. The standard of teaching is very high – the professors and lecturers are interesting speakers and knowledgeable on their subject. My class has such a range of nationalities that it makes the lessons more dynamic, but it also has a real effect on personal development. By being in these classes you develop a more tolerant attitude and change your outlook completely on some things.

'The Hague is a big city which has strong links to the European Union through Europol and the European Court of Justice.

Therefore, anyone with an interest in following a career in the European Union has an advantage by being in this city, as there are many opportunities to get ahead and make connections.

'If you are interested in international affairs, different cultures and experiencing something new and exciting, then I would advise you to think about attending a university abroad. This is one of the best opportunities to learn, live and develop. I can say that this is absolutely the best decision I have made.'

The Hague University of Applied Sciences (www. thehagueuniversity.com) offers a wide range of undergraduate and postgraduate courses taught in English. Its staff and students come from over 135 different countries.

STUDENT CASE STUDY
John Magee, Norway

John Magee decided to study overseas in order to become more competitive in the job market. He is enrolled on an MSc in International Management at the BI Norwegian Business School in Norway.

'I had already received a bachelor's degree in the UK and I thought studying a master's degree overseas would equip me with a number of advantages. After receiving advice from various employers, I discovered that firms would perceive a candidate who chose to study abroad as someone who has made an effort to differentiate themselves from others and who has secured invaluable cultural experiences, which is of ever-growing importance in today's globalised world. Additionally, the prospect of acquiring language skills could only increase my employability.'

There were other factors that also helped him to decide on study abroad. 'I felt the opportunity to live and study in a foreign country would be an adventure; I could kill two birds with one stone, by having a travel-like experience and securing a good degree at the same time. It also did not hurt if I could have easy access to alpine sporting activities that I could never access in the UK.'

John started looking at options across Europe, having already considered the factors that were most important to him and his future. 'Firstly, the schools had to be ranked on the Financial Times European Business School Rankings, so they were internationally recognisable to future employers. Secondly, the schools had to offer my desired degree, in my case, an MSc in international business/international management. Thirdly, a more selfish criterion of being situated in a mountainous country that offered easy access to alpine activities. Lastly, it was preferable if the course offered an exchange semester, to help me secure the maximum amount of international experience.'

John discovered through his research that tuition fees at many European business schools were comparable in price. After narrowing down his choices to a shortlist that included institutions in France, Switzerland, Sweden and Norway, John opted for BI Norwegian Business School, after being offered a scholarship that covered his tuition fees. 'BI stood out from other business schools in this respect. The school offers a range of scholarships based on previous academic performance. The type of scholarship offered varies depending on where you come from, for instance, more substantial scholarships are offered to students from more underprivileged countries. You are required to re-apply each year and your assessment will be based on the grades you have so far achieved at the school.'

John found the university application process fairly straightforward. 'The application process was very simple and relatively hassle free. Everything was done online and they only required a few documents such as my undergraduate transcripts, my CV and some essays I was required to write to apply for a scholarship. A GMAT* score was also required.'

Norway is not an EU country, but there is no need for a visa. 'They do have some checks for European citizens, however, these are minimal and it is simply a matter of registering with the relevant government departments when you arrive.'

John feels that he has been well-supported during the transition to his host country. 'I received a booklet with all the information a student would need; it included accommodation options, part-time employment information, term dates, cultural information, basic Norwegian phrases etc. I have received all the support I could possibly require. There are information meetings when you arrive and a designated international office for any further questions.

'Accommodation can be hard to find, but as long as you are prepared and begin applying early you will find something. The information packs you receive from the university will have details of possible accommodation options. Unfortunately it is not like the UK and the universities do not have their own halls of residence. However, there are student associations such as SIO who have plenty of independent student halls. If possible I would try to avoid a student area called Kringsja. Many international students are directed here and, although it is very cheap, you get what you pay for. However it is located on the doorstep of Oslo's huge forest park with lots of cross-country skiing and mountain biking possibilities.'

John may not have to pay fees, but he has living costs to pay for and Norway is one of the more expensive European countries to live in. 'The cost of living in Norway is significantly higher than most other countries, so I have to be prudent with my living costs if the financial benefits of a scholarship are going to pay off.'

John has plenty of tips for fellow students regarding food. 'Food in Norway is extortionately priced; you must be careful which national supermarket chains you shop at because they vary in price. I recommend Kiwi or Rema 1000 for the best deals. Meat and alcohol are particularly expensive and it may be worthwhile popping over the Swedish border at the start of semester to buy meat in bulk and then freeze it, many Norwegians do this themselves to save money. As for Norwegian food itself, their diet is fairly similar to most northern European countries, meals of meat, potatoes and vegetables seem to be fairly normal. However, Norwegians do often eat some food that we might find strange in the UK. A student's typical lunch will often consist of crackers covered with various fillings from a tube such as caviar or bacon paste, however, this meal is very cheap so worth a try. Norwegian portions are also noticeably smaller than in the UK. It is an absolute must to bring a packed lunch (or *matpakke* in Norwegian) to school with you, it saves you a lot of money and all Norwegians do it.

'Your main expenditures are food and rent and both of these can be substantially cut if you are organised. For instance, shopping at the cheaper supermarkets, buying meat in Sweden and buying alcohol at the duty free can save a surprising amount of money. As for rent there is plenty of attractive student accommodation available and reasonably priced. You may find that social activities will be the real unavoidable expense, avoid buying too many drinks while at bars or clubs or eating out too much. Oslo living expenses could be comparable to living in central London.'

Potential students might be hoping for part-time work to support themselves while they study. Although non-Norwegian EU students have the right to work a certain number of hours per week, the language barrier can limit job opportunities. 'Finding a suitable part-time job may be difficult for non-Norwegian speakers, although American themed restaurants or British and Irish pubs can actually prefer English speakers, so finding work is possible.

'There is a lot to do in your free time and it is easy to get around the country (or into Sweden) by train, bus and plane. If you are an outdoor enthusiast you will love Norway. Norwegians have an affinity with the outdoors and love to camp, ski, cross-country ski, forest run and mountain bike. Nordmarka Forest Park is right on Oslo's doorstep where all these things are easily accessible by public transport, an enviable trait that is unique to Oslo. It is also possible to join hiking associations for almost nothing and with that you get the use of hundreds of fully stocked cabins all over Norway.

'Compared to the UK, it is very noticeable that few international students choose to study full time in Norway. Therefore you may find it difficult finding other students who are in similar situation to yourself and the language barrier can quickly prove problematic. Although Norwegians are proficient in English, they often are still reluctant or embarrassed to speak it unless they have to. This can make the process of getting to know other students slower than in other countries. However, once you get to know them they are great, fun-loving and sporty people.'

John hasn't yet decided on his plans for when the course ends. 'I personally believe English speakers are seriously restricted to getting a graduate job in Norway, however it gives you a good incentive to learn the language whilst there. The most obvious English-speaking industry is the oil industry.'

For John, the experience so far has been positive and one that he highly recommends. 'You will gain experiences, meet people and learn things that would never be possible if you choose to stay at home.'

*__GMAT__, Graduate Management Admission Test, www.mba.com.

BI Norwegian Business School (www.bi.no/en) is a private, independent, specialised university institution and is one of Europe's largest business schools.

STUDENT CASE STUDY
Sema Ali, Italy

Sema Ali was ready for a change, so she decided to enrol in a Bachelor's degree in Economics, Management and Finance at Bocconi University in Milan, Italy. 'I have lived in England all my life and wanted a new experience and complete independence. I considered the United States but decided to go for Italy; I studied Italian as one of my A levels, so by living here I hope to become fluent in Italian. I also think Italy is a beautiful country and not too far from home. My father told me about Bocconi and it was the perfect option for me; it is in Italy and is an excellent university with an outstanding reputation for the course I want to study.'

For Sema, the costs in Italy were much lower than the American colleges and more in line with those in the UK. 'The cost is quite similar, here one can also apply for scholarships and one can get reduced fees if needed.'

The application process was relatively simple. 'I completed the application online and had to send in certain documents. Also, since I did not do the SATs I had to take the Bocconi Admission Test.' In fact, it seems as though the entire process was straightforward and supportive. 'Before I arrived, Bocconi sent various useful emails about the university and Milan, which gave me the information I needed to settle in. When I got to Milan, they arranged various welcome days where information was given to us and there were different desks where we could go to and ask questions on certain matters. Bocconi also organises parties and events, which is a good way to meet people.'

Sema managed to get a place in one of Bocconi's dorms, but lots of people weren't so lucky. 'My advice to potential students is to make sure you fill out the form as early as possible by the date they tell you. Also, if you do not feel that you filled it out early enough, then start to look for apartments. I plan to stay here for a year and then move out into an apartment with some friends.'

She speaks highly of her academic experiences at the university. 'Bocconi is very international with students from all over the world. The classes are taught in English and it is a very broad-based business curriculum. The professors are very knowledgeable and the classes are not very big, unlike schools I considered in the States where some undergraduate classes had hundreds of students in them. The professors are also very friendly and accessible.'

And what does the future hold for Sema? 'I am considering internships for the summer. After university, I plan to work for several years before I apply for an MBA, either at Bocconi or at another university in the States.'

Bocconi University (www.unibocconi.eu) is a private research university of international standing in business, economics and law.

STUDENT CASE STUDY
Fiona Higgins, Finland

Fiona Higgins is studying for a Bachelor's degree in International Hotel, Restaurant & Tourism Management at HAAGA-HELIA, University of Applied Sciences, Finland. She chose to study abroad because she had been living at home in St Andrews, Scotland long enough and wanted a new experience. She was planning to start a degree in international hospitality anyway, when a long-distance relationship made her rethink her plans. 'I chose Finland because my boyfriend is Finnish. The long distance just got far too expensive and it was too hard to have to keep saying goodbye every month.'

It turned out that there were financial benefits to studying in Finland too. 'As I am a European Union student I can study in Finland for free, compared to the £1,500 plus a year in Scotland.'

There are about 14 universities and universities of applied science (or polytechnics) in the Helsinki area. In Finland, universities focus on research-based education, while universities of applied science offer work-related education. Fiona started off by looking into a number of different schools in Helsinki, but excellence in her chosen subject led her to HAAGA-HELIA. 'HAAGA-HELIA was the best for hotel management; it has a strong reputation for this subject, so it was ideal.'

Fiona found the university application process quite different from the system back home. 'It was very different. In the UK you either get the grades they need or not. It's simple. HAAGA-HELIA is a bit different and, from what I understand, it's very similar in other universities in Finland. If you get your school grades and meet the admissions criteria, they put you through to the entrance exam, which includes an English exam. The next step is a group aptitude test and then an interview. This definitely ensures that all the students are serious about studying at this university.'

After receiving her offer, Fiona got lots of support from the institution. 'HAAGA-HELIA were extremely helpful, they were so quick at replying to all my terribly trivial questions and told me everything I had to do in preparation for moving to Finland. Once I got here, they had organised at least three different events for international students, welcoming them to Finland and helping them get around Helsinki and answering all the questions that needed to be answered.' Fiona also used some websites for expats in Finland, which helped her to find out what to expect.

'I didn't need to apply for a visa (being an EU student), however to live in Finland you need to get a social security number, and go to the police station to ask for permission to have the right to reside in Finland. At which point you go to the magistrate office *(maistraatti)*, apply to have residence and your address is submitted.

'I was lucky with accommodation because I am living with my boyfriend, so he sorted that out. HOAS is the student housing organisation, which is meant to be very helpful. The housing is very cheap (cheaper than the UK) and relatively decent. However, the food is expensive, but it's good food, way more healthy than the options you get in the UK.

'Finland is considered to be one of the best countries to live in (*Newsweek*, 2010), the accommodation is reasonable, the university is free for EU students, the only thing that costs a lot is the food and the alcohol, but as long as you are aware of money, then it should work out! For health insurance, you need an EHIC which will cover you for costs at hospitals (up to a certain amount, of course, see www.ehic.org.uk). The public transport is fantastic; it's so easy once you get the hang of it. It is a bit expensive, but you can get a travel card which is worth the money, for sure.'

Fiona has found the approach to teaching at HAAGA-HELIA a little different. 'It feels a little more like school, as the classes are much smaller. It really forces you to concentrate. Also the classes are not the regular one-hour classes, but instead about three hours. I think it's better that way. It means you have more time to learn.'

Fiona feels positive about her move to Finland, but it hasn't all been easy. 'I'm not going to lie, it's not easy at the beginning. I got absolutely lost the first day on the train, but after the first week or two it feels like home. The Finns are hard to get to know, but once you know them they will be the most open people and so caring. The lifestyle is amazing; it's so easy and the social life is ideal for students. But it's not so easy to get a job in Finland if you don't speak Finnish, unless you're alright with doing jobs that don't require the language to start with, like washing dishes.

'Every day brings something new, which means you learn something new every day. It is amazing to explore a city and get to know the people and the ways of life. I would recommend moving from the UK if you can. It might seem scary and daunting, but it is exciting and there are often Brits around to help you out! The people will be good to you if you smile and chat and keep positive. Don't worry, the flights to the UK are cheap too.

'Being at this university and doing this course opens up so many doors and it means that I will be able to work in a decent hotel, I hope. And go back abroad. I am learning Finnish too, which is not going too well, but is going!'

So it turns out that this is only the start of studying abroad for Fiona. 'I plan on heading to Asia with my degree, hopefully China. Leaving and seeing what it is like to live outside of the UK has confirmed my ideas to live away from home.'

HAAGA-HELIA (www.haaga-helia.fi/en) is a university of applied sciences preparing professionals for business and services.

STUDENT CASE STUDY
Esme Leyland, Spain

Esme Leyland was feeling disillusioned with the UK and was in search of something different. She chose to enrol on an LLB Law degree at IE University in Segovia, Spain. 'I haven't seen much of the world (yet) but out of the few countries I have visited, Spain is one of my favourites. Spanish is one of the most widely spoken languages in the world, so to be able to speak Spanish would assist greatly with my chosen career – international commercial law.

'I recognise there is a world of opportunities out there and I aim to experience as many as possible. I researched international universities on Google and IE University came up. It looked amazing. Segovia is the type of town I've always wanted to live in – old, traditional and historical. It also offered business and law combined and is one of the top business schools in the world.'

Studying at a private university comes with a large price tag. 'The price doesn't seem that bad when you consider everything you can gain from studying at IE compared to an English education. Whether you study at Oxford or Nottingham Trent, you would never receive the same level of education as you would at IE.' Esme describes the amount of support that she has received from her university as 'incredible'. She continues, 'The lady who was helping me with my application was great, she was there to answer every question. The whole experience was very personal and helpful.

'Applying to universities in the UK was a chore, one that you dreaded when the time came around. Applying to IE, you were in control, there were no barriers, you could submit more and more information to help with your application, whereas in the UK it is very limited and rigid.' Since she has arrived, Esme has continued to receive a high level of support.

She is also enjoying having her own place to live. 'I like to have my independence, so I could never live in residence. It's nice to be able to cook for yourself, do your own washing, clean your own flat; to have people come and go as you please and feel as if you really are taking the next step in your life, living in your own place and having independence. Living costs can be whatever you make them. If you're sensible with your heating, water, electricity, etc, then they won't be too bad. You've got to learn to make do and make better.'

There have been some negative experiences; Esme highly recommends taking out adequate insurance. 'GET IT! I'm not usually one for insurance, but as soon as I arrived in Madrid all my luggage got stolen, every item to my name, never to be seen again! It was an expensive lesson to learn.'

She is finding plenty of differences in teaching and learning. 'It's international; it's education on a whole different level. I'm not just learning about things relating to the UK anymore, I'm learning about the world. The learning experience is a great one to value. The teaching is also completely different; a lot more laid back, a lot more respect from the professors. Although, it's important to make sure you understand exactly what the professors are saying, as some words can be lost in translation (even in English).'

For Esme, studying abroad is the just the start of her plans to leave the UK. 'For me personally, studying overseas is an achievement. The best thing for me is knowing that I'm not in the UK and I don't need to go back. I am learning so much about the world and what's out there; I'm discovering more and more possibilities. And of course, the best thing is all the different people you interact with on a daily basis, the places these people will take you and the difference they'll make to your life, something you won't necessarily find in the UK.'

IE University (www.ie.edu) is a private university offering its students tailor-made education with an international, humanistic and entrepreneurial perspective.

STUDENT CASE STUDY
Shanna Hanbury, the Netherlands

Shanna Hanbury is studying for a Bachelor's degree in Social Sciences at Amsterdam University College, the Netherlands. She wasn't enjoying her education at the University of Exeter and this prompted her to start looking for opportunities elsewhere. 'I didn't think the courses were particularly engaging or energetic and I need to be in a place that is culturally vibrant and be in a more stimulating academic environment. So after my first year there I started looking into university courses in Europe taught in English, with a focus on interesting cities.

'I decided on Amsterdam because of the university, not the other way around. Small class sizes, a real focus on diversity and an open (liberal arts) degree definitely played a big role in my initial attraction to the institution.'

The cost of studying in the Netherlands compares favourably to the UK. 'Although usually universities in the Netherlands are about €1,700 a year, Amsterdam University College is about double that because you need to pay the tuition fee to the University of Amsterdam and an institutional fee to Amsterdam University College. I suppose the small class sizes and focus on each student make it more expensive to run.'

Shanna found the application process reasonably straightforward. 'I had to write a personal statement and an essay. I was out of Europe when I applied so they did the interview over Skype. They were also fine with me scanning and emailing a lot of the documents, which was a huge help.'

When she arrived, there was support to help her get settled in. 'There's an introduction week before class starts where they help you with a lot of the more bureaucratic things you have to sort out as a non-Dutch student.' She also has staff she can turn to throughout her studies. 'Each person has a tutor that they can go to if they need any help with academic or personal issues. Personally, I haven't needed much support since I've arrived.'

An additional bonus for students new to the Netherlands is the fact that AUC is a residential college, with accommodation guaranteed for the three years of the programme. 'There are three buildings just with students from my uni. It's a bit outside of the city, but in Amsterdam terms that means a 15-minute bike ride away from the centre.'

There are lots of options for eating well, although food isn't cheap. 'Food is very expensive here, definitely more than in the UK. I usually buy fruits and vegetables at the Turkish shops and other things at the supermarket. However, there are also many squats around the city which work like social and cultural centres where they have three-course vegan dinners for close to nothing, usually one or two nights a week and all run by volunteers.

'There are always a lot of gigs happening and exhibition opening events which have free drinks, music, great art and can be quite fun to attend. That being said, Amsterdam is not like London or Berlin. It's smaller and has a village feel to it. If you go out late on a Tuesday night, chances are the city will be dead, but overall there's a great balance between it being a quiet, safe place and still a vibrant, culturally active place.'

Shanna is particularly enjoying her educational experiences at Amsterdam University College. 'The maximum class size is 25 people and no evaluation can be more than 25% of your final grade, which breaks it up nicely. Teaching is definitely more personal and energetic, the students are engaged in the classes and there is a lot more discussion-based learning.'

She reflects on her experience of studying abroad: 'I don't think that the fact that it's overseas makes it good, Amsterdam as a city and Amsterdam University College as an institution and all the lovely people I've met here are what make it great.'

Amsterdam University College (www.auc.nl) is a joint excellence initiative of the University of Amsterdam and VU University Amsterdam. It is a selective liberal arts and sciences university programme offering interdisciplinary education in small classes.

STUDENT CASE STUDY
Stuart Bramley, USA

Footballer Stuart Bramley had always wanted to study in the USA. He managed to secure a scholarship to Scottsdale Community College in Arizona on their General Studies course. Studying in the USA allows him to gain a degree and continue playing soccer, while also benefiting from good financial support.

He liked Scottsdale because of the support they could offer him and because of the size of the institution. 'They were fantastic and offered lots of close support. As it is a small college, they can work on a one-to-one basis with students.'

Stuart acknowledges the challenges of applying. 'The application process was long; however, I worked closely with the international student adviser to make it all happen, once I had established where I was going. My next step was to go to the US Embassy to get my visa and I-20. This was a nerve-racking process as I didn't want to get told I wasn't allowed to go. I had to travel down to London. I prepared by studying what I was going to be questioned about. If you answered wrong, you might not be allowed to enter the country.'

He was not alone in navigating this process. 'I got a lot of support from Scottsdale. They helped me with what was on the visa, questions, and everything else in order to get here. Since I have arrived in the States, I have had one-to-one support from the international student adviser who was fantastic in setting up my schedule and what I was going to study. We have built up a very close relationship, which makes me feel good being so far away from home.'

Stuart's experience of education at Scottsdale has been quite different from his time in the UK. 'You have to stick at it hard otherwise you will get dropped from your classes and not allowed to study. It really gives you an incentive to get good grades.'

He has found himself somewhere to live off campus. 'Living off campus is nice if you find good apartments. These can be relatively cheap when you are living with a group of students.' He estimates that accommodation costs are 'about $700 to $900 (£450 to £580) per month, including water and electricity. However, if there is a group of you, you only end up paying a few hundred each, which (with the exchange rate) works out cheap.' Living in self-catered accommodation also means that Stuart has the freedom to shop for his own food and control his diet, as required when playing competitive sport.

Stuart hasn't found it too hard to adjust to his new life overseas. 'Being away from home is hard for anyone at some point, but I have a good group of friends and support from the college.' He is really enjoying life in the States. 'It is brilliant fun; a different lifestyle and culture altogether. It's just a whole different experience regarding people and the way of life. It's very social.'

The US system of health insurance has been a change for Stuart. 'I find insurance is a little bit of a hassle as I have to claim back what I use. For instance, if I go to the doctor I have to pay first and then claim back what I spend.' He gets around the area using his bike and the bus, but lots of his friends drive. (You can get a driving licence from the age of 16 in the USA.)

After his studies, Stuart would like to play professional soccer or find work. He would highly recommend the opportunity to study in the USA. 'It is such a different lifestyle and culture, a new experience that is fun and amazing; a brand new eye-opening life.'

Scottsdale Community College (www.scottsdalecc.edu) is a two-year college which has transfer agreements with a number of private and public universities, enabling progression to bachelor's degrees.

STUDENT CASE STUDY
Simon McCabe, USA

After completing his first degree and a master's degree in the
UK, Simon McCabe started looking for a position as a teaching
or research assistant or for a place on a PhD. After applying
for over 50 positions with no success, he started to look further
afield to Europe and the USA. He ended up gaining a place on a
PhD in Social Psychology at University of Missouri in the USA.

'I didn't pick the country so much as the country picked me.
I could not afford to fund a PhD out of my own pocket so the
financial support and waivers I have received are a necessity to
me. I found that a lot of the universities I was applying to in the
UK did not offer the financial support that I could find in the
USA.'

Money wasn't the only factor for Simon; academic expertise
played a large part too. 'I'm researching in an area called terror
management theory and there are more researchers, professors
and articles existing in the USA than there are in the UK.

'I was interested in learning about American culture and
spending some time abroad to experience more of the world. I
believe that the combination of academic progression and cultural
exploration can enhance the experience of graduate school.'

Simon realised that good research is key when deciding where to
study. 'I applied to five universities in the USA and reached the
interview stage of two of those. I made my choice based on my
impression of my potential advisers and their publication record,
as well as information attained from their current graduate
students. I did some rather intense research, checking out the
university website, the city website and the online literature
available. I also used more creative methods such as searching

for YouTube videos of the campus and the city, listening to the local radio station online and reading the local paper online to try to get a better grip of what my future life might be like.'

The university application process required a lot of work. 'Applying to a US university is not the same as applying to a UK university. I spent a whole year preparing my application, as recommended by the Fulbright Commission. I found out I would need to take the GRE (requiring a trip to London)*, three letters of recommendation and a personal statement, alongside some sample work. When you multiply that to accommodate the five universities I wanted to apply to it mounts up and time disappears fast.'

Simon did more than just complete the applications; he started to build up a relationship with his potential department. 'I honestly think that the most important part of my application wasn't in any of these materials requested by the university. I was emailing back and forth with potential advisers over a period of eight months and feel that this dialogue can greatly swing favour in your direction if you can put forward some ideas and get a handle on what the department is looking for in its applicants.'

After gaining an offer of a place, the next big hurdle is to get a visa. 'Applying for a visa is tedious, anxiety-inducing and confusing, at first. You will need to travel to London and wait for hours at the US Embassy with hundreds of other people. You will need to take part in an interview (which in my case was extremely brief, but I have read horror stories online of problematic utterances leading to further probing). The online website will cause you a headache but if you approach it as just a hurdle to jump you can dismiss a lot of the worry. After you receive your visa you will need it upon entry to the USA and then again for opening accounts etc. After this you should store it carefully. Be aware of things that may impact on it, for example, if you decide to travel or get a job.'

Simon had plenty of help from his university before he travelled to Missouri. 'The international centre had me sign up to their mailing list early and sent regular updates on things I should expect and interviews with previous international students with tips and suggestions for places to get furniture, to eat and seek help if required. If your university does have an international centre, check out the website to get some really helpful info.'

The support has continued since his arrival. 'The university does a great job of providing students with all that they need, be they international or not. This includes support for filing taxes and opportunities for employment.'

In spite of all his research and the support available, Simon did face some difficulties adjusting and he has had some negative experiences. 'My girlfriend came here after two months of my arrival with the plan for her to stay. Unfortunately, due to US laws this was impossible. After one month of talking to lawyers and exhausting other resources she returned to England and we ended our relationship. This was a particularly hard first semester for me and may have contributed to some adjustment issues.'

He hasn't yet decided what he will do or where he will go after he finishes his studies. 'At the moment I am not sure what country I will end up in, it depends on life events – if a parent gets ill and requires care or if I meet a love interest here; all those things that you can't predict. But I will hopefully be getting a tenure track job as an assistant professor.'

For Simon the best thing about studying overseas has been his personal experiences. 'I like that when I walk out of my office at the end of the day, when the books are back on the shelf and the computer has whirled down to shut off that I continue learning and experiencing new people, places and culture. For me it's about seeing the world and I think that the personal experiences you have are as important as the academic experience you attain at any institute.'

Simon has plenty of tips for would-be students. 'Look early for accommodation! I had 20 sheets of A4 paper on my wall with the name, online rating, price, distance to campus, distance to bus stop, distance to the mall and pool/gym/laundry/utilities listed. I then closed out the options that were unsuitable and I have a great place. Whilst others have moved into new places I do not think I will move in my remaining four years. Apartment Finder (www.apartmentfinder.com) is your friend.

'Just try the food. If you don't like it you don't have to have it again. Remember to tip. Cook stuff from your own country to feed to American friends, they will love you.

'Get insurance. Although I have had no problems yet I would dread it and kick myself if something broke, was stolen or damaged which I could not afford to replace.

'Budget: keep an eye on your accounts and do a monthly forecast. Be aware you may not be able to take out credit cards or loans immediately on arrival, as you need to build a credit rating.

'Usually the head of department will have a list of available opportunities for financial support and scholarships. Get in touch with them and even if they don't they can point you in the right direction. Otherwise Google, Google, Google.

'I wouldn't recommend working while studying if you can help it (during a graduate course). Summer, winter and spring break may give you some more free time than usual but it can damage your academic productivity. Even 20 hours a week will nibble into important school-oriented pursuits.

'Adapting to the lifestyle and culture has been difficult for me. I have been here for one year and sometimes feel alienated from US culture. Sometimes I have even felt like derogating the culture and find certain behaviours or patterns of speech annoying. This is to be expected. There is a careful balancing game you must play between holding on to your identity and getting by in a new environment. I always remind myself that it ultimately comes down to respect. You are in someone else's country and you must respect their way of doing things. This does not mean you need to be submissive to the culture. The US government have made available a PDF on one of their websites for tackling this psychological issue and recognise the challenges of incoming students from other countries. (Lots of university websites have this information, along with YouTube clips on dealing with culture shock.) You would think that being from the UK and going to the USA wouldn't be that big of a shock; you'd be wrong. You will be confused, surprised and shocked on a day-to-day basis for at least five months. And these things still crop up later on.

'Think about options for after you finish your studies from time to time. Do you want to stay in your country of study or move back home; perhaps you want to move to yet another country? Factor in distance from relatives, relationship partners, cost of living, language barriers, cultural attractiveness and opportunities for career progression. I would suggest not waiting until the last year of your degree to do this but have it as an ongoing conversation with yourself as you continue to explore and learn.'

***GRE** is now available as a paper-based test in Leeds and Kent. Computer-based tests are offered in London, Birmingham, Edinburgh, Leeds, Manchester, Peterborough and Dublin. See www.gre.org for details.

University of Missouri (www.missouri.edu) is a public research university and a member of the Association of American Universities (an association of 61 leading research universities in the USA and Canada). It is ranked number 12 in the Times Higher Education World University Rankings 2011/2012.

STUDENT CASE STUDY
Alex Warren, Canada

It was while studying for an international baccalaureate (IB) at an international school in the UK that Alex Warren started wondering about studying overseas. He gained a place at the University of British Columbia in Canada to study geography. 'I was constantly around people from different places and wanted a chance to explore a different culture and lifestyle.' He chose Canada because of the opportunities to ski, the beautiful surroundings and because it is an English-speaking country. While he was applying, he received the support of a peer adviser whom he could email with questions or problems.

He pays tuition fees of around C$8,000 (£5,000) per semester, more than he would have paid in the UK. 'Now that the fees in the UK have gone up the difference is much less. I received an entrance scholarship and a second scholarship in my second year. There is a student financial centre if you are struggling and you automatically get put forward for certain scholarships if you are eligible. Vancouver is not a cheap city; cafeteria food in residence is not cheap but you get discounted meal plans which make it more affordable.'

He has encountered some differences in the education system. 'We have midterm exams and many smaller assignments due throughout the year. School also goes all year round if you want it to, although most people don't take classes in the summer semester. It works on a credit system and each class you take is worth a certain amount of credits (usually three). You have to obtain a certain amount of credits to gain your degree. You also have to take certain subjects, for example a language, a science and an English subject. Coming from the background of the IB,

I liked the breadth of study, but it is a good point to note in case
you are not interested in other disciplines.'

Alex has some tips for other students who may be considering
Canada.

- 'Go into residence first year. You meet loads of people
  and if you have a good support network it's much easier
  to settle in.'
- 'Some foods are much more expensive than the UK, but
  the sushi is cheap and amazing!'
- 'You should get a Medical Services Plan (MSP medical
  insurance) that costs around C$60 (£37) per month,
  then you are covered for all eventualities.'
- 'Getting around Vancouver is easy. The transit system
  is amazing and you get a bus pass included in your
  tuition. You can also take advantage of Greyhound
  buses going to the States and cheap deals to Mexico.'
- 'There are amazing winter sports here and so many
  mountains! There is also amazing nightlife, but
  drinking is much more expensive than England.'

One challenge has been adjusting to the time difference,
particularly when he wants to contact friends and family back
home. 'It is pretty tricky scheduling Skype dates with England.'
However, that hasn't been enough of an issue to put him off
staying on in Canada after he finishes his studies. 'I would like
to stay here and get a job. I have contacts in my department and
would like to use them to go into urban planning or
water management. In the future I may consider graduate
school.'

Alex would recommend his experiences of overseas study. 'I
honestly feel like I have broadened my horizons. If I had stayed in
England, I would never have considered the possibility of living

or working abroad. Now I have the option to stay here, to return to England or go to the States.'

University of British Columbia (www.ubc.ca) has a student population of 50,000 and holds an international reputation for excellence in advanced research and learning. It is ranked number 22 in the Times Higher Education World University Rankings 2011/2012.

STUDENT CASE STUDY
Kadie O'Byrne, Australia

Kadie O'Byrne is studying for a BSc BVMS in Veterinary Medicine and Surgery at Murdoch University in Perth, Australia. She chose to study there for the experience. 'Having visited Australia before, I loved the place; I know how hard it can be to move out here, so I thought studying here would open doors and allow me to stay here if I decided to. Additionally, studying veterinary medicine, the diversity of animals out in Australia is much more copious than that of the UK.'

She decided on the city of Perth partly because it is a smaller city. 'I also could have gone to Melbourne, but being from a small island like Jersey, I felt Melbourne's size would completely overpower me and be too big of a change. Moving across the world was a big enough change already without making it harder.'

Kadie took advantage of some assistance to navigate the application process. 'I went through Study Options. They were fantastic and made the process so easy. They copied all of my transcripts for my A level results and sent off passport, results, organised the visa, the course, everything! They were so great.

It happened relatively quickly too, it was only about two months from applying to getting an answer. Although I had to wait six months until I could start as here we start in February, unlike the UK where it is September.'

She describes the visa application as 'a lot of paperwork and very tedious', although help from Study Options made things easier. 'They told me all the things I needed, got the right documents and sent everything off for me, so it was a lot easier than one would first expect.'

Kadie then started to get support from her university. 'They sent information packs about the uni and the course and put me in touch with people co-ordinating my course. They also sorted me with accommodation in the student village.'

As an international student, she feels well looked after. 'They run international outings to meet other students and discuss how you are coping with being so far from home. Additionally in the vet programme we are all assigned an academic adviser. Their role is to meet with you every term and discuss your progress or problems with courses, lectures and also personal problems. It is a great system. However for those that need more help, the uni offers a free counselling service too.'

She finds education in Australia quite different from the UK. 'It seems to be more personal. Our lecturers are great, we are on a first name basis and they are so approachable and very friendly. They really try to get to know you and give you great feedback on assignments and how you're going throughout the year.'

Like many international students, Kadie did miss her friends and family back home. 'For the first six months to a year, I struggled with homesickness. Living in the uni village really helped, having people in the same situation as you gives you someone to talk to and exchange ways to make you feel less homesick. Plus in the first year you are so busy having fun and meeting new people, time does fly and you don't have much time to feel homesick.

'Skype really helped. At first, I would Skype my mum nearly every day, although the time difference was a challenge. Now I Skype her once a week. However, three years down and I still have my days of homesickness. But I always tell people that you never stop getting homesick, you just learn to live and cope with the feeling. And it does get easier!'

Australia isn't a cheap option for UK students, with tuition fees and costs of living higher than in the UK, although there are some scholarship opportunities. 'Scholarships are open for international students and they vary between courses, Emails and posters go out around uni when options to apply come up.

'I would say clothes are cheaper here, but eating out and food shopping is more than one would expect in the UK. At first, I was working with the pound and converting everything, but once you start earning the dollar it becomes relative, so I stopped.'

The great lifestyle is one of Australia's selling points. 'It is so much better than the UK. The weather is fantastic – a little hot in summer at first, but you get used to it. It's such an outdoor lifestyle with bbqs all the time, fantastic beaches and the culture is awesome. People are so friendly and you will never feel lost in Perth. There's so much to do, there are always markets around and outdoor festivals.'

Kadie shares her tips for coping with living on the other side of the world.

- 'For the first year, definitely stay in the uni village. It helps you meet people and find out what is around you. Also, living with people really helps take your mind off the homesickness.'

- 'It is a requirement with the visa to have overseas health insurance. When you go to the doctor or get a prescription or hospital treatment, you just send your receipts off like any other insurance claim. You get some (but not all of it) back, but every little helps when you are a student.'
- 'I felt it helped to get a job for food and shopping expenses, rather than bug my parents more. There is plenty of opportunity. I have worked as a bartender, waitress and now in a vet practice, but there are so many options and a great community supporting students so you will not struggle to find a job.'

Kadie has decided that she would like to stay on in Australia after she finishes her course. 'Visa options are complicated. There is a lot of detail about staying afterwards that you need to look into depending on your situation. But it is possible. I am hoping to stay and work as a vet here in Perth, but I would also like to see other parts of Australia. I plan on taking a year or so to travel and see different places to find the part of Australia I truly want to live in. One thing I do know is that I most definitely want to stay and live in Australia.'

On top of all the other things Kadie loves about her experience, she feels that studying abroad has helped her to grow as a person. 'I found it really brought me out of my shell. You are alone in a city thousands of miles away from home – you learn to be outgoing, talk to people and do things. It has been such an experience living here and such a better way of life than in the UK. You meet so many people that will stay friends for life and see things you otherwise would not have seen and experienced in the UK. Take a leap and do it! You will never look back!'

Murdoch University (www.murdoch.edu.au) is a research-intensive university where free thinking and a flexible approach to learning is encouraged.

STUDENT CASE STUDY
Warren Mitty, China

Warren Mitty is a BSc Building Engineering Management
student at Loughborough University and took advantage of
the opportunity to study for part of his degree at Hong Kong
Polytechnic University. 'I decided to study overseas to experience
new cultures and ways of living, to meet new friends and to
witness new styles of teaching to further my education. I also
hoped to broaden my horizons of the Far East.'

He found the online application process to be straightforward,
receiving all the help he needed from the International Affairs
Office at his university in Hong Kong.

As an exchange student, Warren continues to pay fees to his
university in the UK, but he has found student life cheap in Hong
Kong. 'Living costs are low, however you must be reasonable
with your spending. There are expensive places and cheap places,
therefore you need to know where to eat and drink at low cost.
You meet local students who show you "off the tourist track"
locations where it is cheap to eat and drink.

'Food in halls is cheap and suitable; however the accommodation
is also situated in an area full of good and cheap local
restaurants. Accommodation is small (this is Hong Kong after
all, where space is in short supply); however you get used to it,
and it is all the space you need. Everything you need is provided
for in the student halls and you meet lots of new friends within
the hall community.'

Warren hasn't experienced any major challenges in adjusting to
life overseas. 'The locals and students are very friendly and the
student halls and university are very helpful in all aspects. There

are schemes set up by the university to help you adjust to life such as the buddy scheme and family scheme, as well as various trips and networking evenings.'

Warren has relished the experience and speaks highly about his international exchange. 'Witnessing a whole new way of life is the best thing about studying overseas, as well as the many friends you will make from all areas of the world and the new places and experiences which you will remember for the rest of your life.'

Hong Kong Polytechnic University (www.polyu.edu.hk) is the largest government-funded tertiary institution in Hong Kong and specialises in professional education.

STUDENT CASE STUDY
William Perkins, South Africa

William Perkins is studying for a Bachelor's degree in History, Politics and Spanish at the University of Cape Town in South Africa.

'When asking people who were completing their undergraduate degree in the UK whether they were enjoying their time, I never received an answer that held any more enthusiasm than "alright", "OK", "not bad". There was a hugely apparent lack of passion, enjoyment, and excitement. I thought that there would be no harm in thinking outside the box and doing something different. So, I decided to come to South Africa because nobody else had. Studying overseas seemed such an attractive option; experiencing new cultures, meeting completely different people, and enjoying the lifestyle of another country.'

Will was attracted by South Africa's rich history and vibrant political culture, particularly relevant to his chosen subjects, history and politics. He was also keen on the different lifestyle that he could live. 'Cape Town is one of the most beautiful and energetic places the world has to offer. There is a zest for life here that those in the UK seem commonly devoid of. Always willing and wanting to be outside, appreciating what surrounds them, and constantly active, the South African exuberance and way of life are a joy to be around. A completely new experience and the idea of pleasant weather, beaches, vineyards, sport, and diverse cultures seemed more attractive than a mere continuation of school.

'University of Cape Town (UCT) is considered by many to be the leading light in tertiary education within Africa. Knowing that I wanted to go abroad, with South Africa a hugely appealing country, there seemed no doubt in my mind about choosing UCT.'

Will applied directly to UCT on a paper-based form. 'It was a little frustrating that there wasn't an electronic way of applying, but there was very little hassle in dealing with forms. I was in constant contact with the Admissions department, who were very helpful and the university got back to me in good time to tell me that my application was successful.'

Getting a visa was also fairly straightforward. 'The visa application requires numerous supporting documents, which I had to sort out in good time before applying. They included medical reports, tuberculosis clearance X-rays, proof of sufficient funds etc. The process of being issued a visa once I had lodged the application was about three weeks. UCT advised me on what I would need in order to be granted a study permit. They were often in contact with me and replied to any questions I had with clarity and speed.'

He has been happy with the support he has continued to receive from his university. 'They have been very accommodating. Due to the diverse nature of Cape Town itself, UCT is very welcoming of foreign students, whether they are studying for a semester-abroad programme or completing their whole degree there.'

He has found the costs of study to be comparable to the UK (at a time when maximum fees were around £3,000). 'The cost of studying at UCT is almost identical to the UK, if not a little cheaper, even before the increase in tuition fees in the UK. There is no student loan system, and you cannot apply for a student loan in the UK and then take it to South Africa, so you need to be self-sufficient economically.'

Will's timetable looked a little different from that of his friends at home. 'I had almost three times the amount of lectures than friends who were studying the same degree in the UK. There are, occasionally, some language difficulties, due to the fact that English is not the mother tongue of some lecturers. However, for the most part, it was a very good institution in terms of lecturing and content.'

Although he didn't have any challenges adjusting to life in South Africa, there were some negative experiences. 'I had one instance of crime, but I was in the wrong place at the wrong time, as can happen in any city worldwide. The negative connotations South Africa has in terms of crime are hugely inflated, I feel.'

Alongside his studies, Will also had the opportunity to gain some work experience while he was there. 'I worked as a hockey and cricket coach at a local secondary school for two years, which was fantastic. It was great to coach the kids and to earn some money at the same time.'

When his studies come to an end, Will will be moving country yet again. 'I am returning to the UK briefly and then going to Italy and Spain to further my learning of the respective languages. My desire to stay in the UK has dwindled hugely since studying abroad, as it has opened my eyes to a far greater and in some ways more exciting world.'

Will loves the reaction he gets when he tells others about his experiences. 'The best thing about studying abroad is seeing people currently studying in the UK being amazed that I decided to study overseas, and wishing that they had done the same thing. I have had a completely different experience than those who stayed in the UK, and I wouldn't change it for anything.'

University of Cape Town (www.uct.ac.za) is a research-led university offering qualifications that are internationally recognised and locally applicable. It is ranked at 103 in the Times Higher Education World University Rankings 2011/2012.

VU University Amsterdam

VU University Amsterdam is a leading European research university established in 1880. With more than 24,000 students and about 4,500 staff we are a modern organisation at the cutting edge of academic higher education. VU University Amsterdam offers a wide range of English-taught programmes at three levels; bachelor's (BA, BSc), master's (MA, MSc) and doctoral (PhD). Twelve faculties share a single campus and cover a wide spectrum of arts, sciences and medicine. We have 14 interdisciplinary research institutes.

VU University Amsterdam is a campus university, located in one of the most dynamic and fast-growing business districts in the Netherlands. We offer outstanding education and research. Amsterdam is the most cultural city in the world, boasting 179 different nationalities, where English is widely spoken.

At VU University Amsterdam some 78 nationalities work and study closely creating a vibrant international academic community. Generally speaking, the teaching style can be described as student-centred: we stimulate students to develop their own opinion through independent and creative thinking. At VU University Amsterdam this means that teaching is conducted in small tutorials, where interactivity is the norm rather than the exception. At all turns, students are invited to question the professors.

To find out more, visit our website at www.vuamsterdam.com.

Case study

This wonderful university is becoming more international year by year

Ting Yang (Beijing, China) Master's in Business Administration

'I look back on my time at VU as the most precious experience of my life. I graduated in 2005 with a Master's degree in Business Administration. At VU, I participated in my first consulting team, and sold my first consulting project to the Amsterdam Canal company. At VU, you will not only be taught from books, but they also give you opportunities to experience the real business world. Lectures are given by professors as well as alumni who are at interesting positions in related fields. Besides knowledge, you can also gain valuable networking skills and build up relationships. You cannot imagine how irreplaceable this can be for your future career.

'Furthermore, I also would like to tell you that this wonderful university is becoming more international year by year. More and more international students visit VU University Amsterdam, and there are more and more exchange opportunities to different countries. Most important of all, at VU I started to understand how to be an individual myself, with self-confidence and respect. I learned how to live independently, how to cope with strange things in daily life. Thanks, my university. I love Amsterdam!'

HAN University of Applied Sciences

Hogeschool ◆ van Arnhem en Nijmegen
HAN University of Applied Sciences

HAN University of Applied Sciences is one of the largest providers of education in the Netherlands, with more than 29,000 students and almost 2,500 staff members spread over two campuses. With more than 3,000 international students, HAN excels at putting theory into practice in an international context throughout all four years of undergraduate study. Spread over the cities of Arnhem and Nijmegen close to the German border, HAN has modern buildings, state-of-the art multimedia centres, world-class laboratories and wireless internet access.

By following a bachelor's course at HAN University of Applied Sciences, students obtain a degree that will be an asset to any employee anywhere in the world. Fully accredited by the Dutch Ministry of Education and internationally recognised, the HAN bachelor's diploma is the starting point of graduates' successful careers and further studies in an international postgraduate programme.

At HAN University of Applied Sciences students benefit from the experience and knowledge of foreign lecturers and international companies. Independence is stimulated and initiative rewarded by providing students with the opportunity to spend part of their education in more than one country. Students attend lectures in the Netherlands, do their work placement abroad, study at partner universities anywhere in the world and do their graduation assignment for an international company.

To maximise the learning process, classes are held only in English and in small groups of a maximum of 30 students, facilitating individual contact with teachers and fellow students. At HAN, personal development is just as important as professional education, therefore student guidance is offered throughout all four years of study. Joining the international student body means merging education with social networks. In the dynamic HAN community students are the heart of a multitude of activities: city trips, parties, thematic weeks, etc.

The Faculty of Engineering and Arnhem Business School, two renowned institutes within HAN University of Applied Sciences, provide international courses in three different fields. At the Faculty of Engineering students can follow the Automotive Engineering and Life Sciences undergraduate programmes, while Arnhem Business School offers undergraduate programmes in business: Business Management Studies (HRQM), International Business and Management Studies, Finance and Control, Communication and Logistics Management (Economics).

British students of HAN University of Applied Sciences pay a yearly tuition fee of €1,771, are only a one-hour flight away from the UK and do not need a visa for the Netherlands. More information about course content and admission requirements can be found on www.han.nl/english.

The world is yours ... go international!

Case study

Amanda Hidayat (Indonesia)

'I really enjoyed my time at Arnhem Business School, I had fantastic classmates, great teaching staff, as well as a great academic and diverse cultural experience. It was a truly satisfying and enriching university experience.'

Further research

Before you go

Direct.gov (Studying at an overseas university)
www.direct.gov.uk/en/BritonsLivingAbroad/EducationAndJobs/
DG_071571

UK Council for International Student Affairs (UKCISA), Country
Contacts
www.ukcisa.org.uk/ukstudent/country_contacts.php

Prospects Country Profiles (postgraduate focus)
www.prospects.ac.uk/country_profiles.htm

UK National Academic Recognition and Information Centre
(NARIC)
www.naric.org.uk
Information on the equivalence of international qualifications

National Contact Point for Professional Qualifications in the
United Kingdom (UKNCP)
www.ukncp.org.uk

Department of Business, Innovation & Skills (BIS)
www.bis.gov.uk/policies/higher-education/access-to-professions/
professional-bodies

Foreign and Commonwealth Office

www.fco.gov.uk

Find an embassy or seek travel advice by country

iAgora

www.iagora.com/studies

Students review and rate their international universities

Association of Commonwealth Universities

www.acu.ac.uk

Citizens Advice

www.citizensadvice.org.uk

For information on how studying overseas might affect your status in the UK

HM Revenue and Customs

www.hmrc.gov.uk

Information on tax when you return to the UK

International course search

Find a master's/MBA/PhD

www.findamasters.com

www.findanmba.com

www.findaphd.com

International Graduate

www.internationalgraduate.net

Search for postgraduate opportunities worldwide

International university league tables

The Times Higher Education World University Rankings

www.timeshighereducation.co.uk/world-university-rankings

QS Top Universities
www.topuniversities.com/university-rankings

Academic Ranking of World Universities
www.arwu.org/

Financial Times Business School Rankings
http://rankings.ft.com/businessschoolrankings/rankings

Costs and funding

Numbeo
www.numbeo.com
Cost of living comparison

Career Development Loans
www.direct.gov.uk/en/EducationAndLearning/AdultLearning/
FinancialHelpForAdultLearners/CareerDevelopmentLoans/index.
htm

International Student Identity Card (ISIC)
www.isic.org
Student discounts worldwide

Student Finance England
www.studentfinance.direct.gov.uk

Student Awards Agency for Scotland
www.saas.gov.uk

Student Finance Wales
www.studentfinancewales.co.uk

Student Finance Northern Ireland
www.studentfinanceni.co.uk

Marie Curie Scheme

www.ukro.ac.uk/mariecurie/Pages/index.aspx

Fellowships and grants for research

Commonwealth Scholarships & Fellowships

www.acu.ac.uk/study_in_the_commonwealth/study

Insurance

European Health Insurance Card (EHIC)

www.ehic.org.uk

Endsleigh Insurance

www.endsleigh.co.uk/Travel/Pages/study-abroad-insurance.aspx

STA Travel Insurance

www.statravel.co.uk/study-abroad-travel-insurance.htm

Blogs & diaries

Third Year Abroad, The Mole Diaries

www.thirdyearabroad.com/before-you-go/the-mole-diaries.html

Samuel Knight in Groningen

http://stkstudyinginholland.tumblr.com

Residence Abroad Blogs (University of Manchester)

www.llc.manchester.ac.uk/undergraduate/residence-abroad/blogs/

Maastricht Students

http://maastricht-students.com/catriona/2011/07/04/21-tips-to-survive-ucm-for-uk-students

Short-term study overseas

Study China

http://servalan.humanities.manchester.ac.uk/studychina

IAESTE
www.iaeste.org

Fulbright Commission
www.fulbright.co.uk
Summer schools at US universities

EducationUSA
www.educationusa.info/pages/students/research-short.php#.
TotkAHLhdQg
Short-term exchanges in the USA

Distance learning
International Council for Open and Distance Education (ICDE)
www.icde.org

Study Portals (search for a distance learning course in Europe)
www.studyportals.eu

Distance Education and Training Council (USA)
www.detc.org/search_schools.php

Educational agents and marketing consultancies
A Star Future
www.astarfuture.co.uk

Study Options
www.studyoptions.com

Degrees Ahead
www.degreesahead.co.uk

Mayflower Education Consultants
www.mayflowereducation.co.uk

PFL Education
www.preparationforlife.com

M & D Europe
www.readmedicine.com

Pass 4 Soccer Scholarships
www.pass4soccer.com

Admissions tests

Scholastic Assessment Test: SAT
http://sat.collegeboard.org

American College Test: ACT
www.act.org

Undergraduate Medicine and Health Sciences Admission Test:
UMAT
http://umat.acer.edu.au

International Student Admissions Test: ISAT
http://isat.acer.edu.au

Special Tertiary Admissions Test: STAT
www.acer.edu.au/tests/stat

Graduate Management Admission Test: GMAT
www.mba.com

Graduate Record Exam: GRE
www.gre.org

Dental Admissions Test: DAT
www.ada.org/dat.aspx

Law School Admissions Test: LSAT

http://lsat.org

Medical College Admission Test: MCAT

www.aamc.org

Graduate Australian Medical Schools Admissions Test: GAMSAT

www.gamsat.acer.edu.au

Health Professions Admission Test (Ireland): HPAT

www.hpat-ireland.acer.edu.au

Studying in Europe

Study Portals

www.studyportals.eu

Search for courses and scholarships in Europe

PLOTEUS (Portal on Learning Opportunities throughout the
European Space)

http://ec.europa.eu/ploteus/home.jsp?language=en

GES Database

www.study-info.eu/index.htm

Search for courses taught in English

EURAXESS

http://ec.europa.eu/euraxess

Research opportunities in the EU

PromoDoc

www.promodoc.eu/study-in-the-eu

Doctoral study in the EU

European Commission, University in Europe
http://ec.europa.eu/youreurope/citizens/education/university

European Commission, Study in Europe
http://ec.europa.eu/education/study-in-europe

Eurodesk
www.eurodesk.org.uk
Information on European work, study, travel and volunteering

Europass
http://europass.cedefop.europa.eu
Documents to make your qualification and skills easily
understood across Europe (CVs, diploma supplements and so on)

Erasmus
www.britishcouncil.org/erasmus-about-erasmus.htm

Erasmus Mundus
http://ec.europa.eu/education/external-relation-programmes/
doc72_en.htm

Austria
www.oead.at/welcome_to_austria/education_research/EN

Belgium
www.highereducation.be (Flemish community)
www.studyinbelgium.be (French community)

Cyprus
www.highereducation.ac.cy/en
www.trncpio.org (Turkish Republic of Northern Cyprus)

Czech Republic
www.studyin.cz
www.msmt.cz (Scholarships)

Denmark

www.studyindenmark.dk

www.optagelse.dk/vejledninger/english/index.html (Danish Co-ordinated Application System, KOT)

www.su.dk/English/Sider/equalstatuseurules.aspx (State Educational Support, SU)

Estonia

www.studyinestonia.ee

Finland

www.studyinfinland.fi

www.universityadmissions.fi (applications to university)

www.admissions.fi (applications to polytechnic or university of applied sciences)

France

www.campusfrance.org/en

www.cnous.fr (National Centre for University & Student Welfare, student life and student costs)

Germany

www.study-in.de/en

www.hochschulkompass.de (Hochschul Kompass, institution search)

www.daad.de (German Academic Exchange Services, DAAD)

www.uni-assist.de/index_en.html (uni-assist, application service for international students)

Hungary

www.studyhungary.hu

Ireland

www.educationireland.ie

www.hetac.ie (Higher Education and Training Awards Council)

www.icosirl.ie (Irish Council for International Students)

www.qualifax.ie (course search)

http://postgradireland.com (postgraduate search)

www.cao.ie (Central Applications Office)

www.pac.ie (Postgraduate Applications Centre)

Italy

www.study-in-italy.it

Latvia

www.studyinlatvia.lv/en

Lithuania

www.smpf.lt/en/studyinlt/about_lithuania

www.skvc.lt/en/content.asp?id=235 (Lithuanian Centre for Quality Assessment in Higher Education)

Netherlands

www.nuffic.nl/international-students

www.studyinholland.co.uk

http://info.studielink.nl/en/studenten/Pages/Default.aspx (Studielink for applications)

www.ib-groep.nl/International_visitors/EU_EEA_students/Grant_for_tuition_or_course_fees.asp

(Department of Education, grants and loans)

Norway

www.studyinnorway.no

www.nokut.no (Norwegian Agency for Quality Assurance in HE, NOKUT)

Poland

www.studyinpoland.pl

Portugal
www.dges.mctes.pt/DGES/pt (General Directorate for HE)

Slovakia
www.studyin.sk

Slovenia
www.slovenia.si/en/study

Switzerland
www.crus.ch/information-programme/study-in-switzerland.
html?L=2

Spain
www.universidad.es/home_en/lang.en
www.educacion.es (Ministry of Education)
www.uned.es (UNED, for evaluation of qualifications)

Sweden
www.studyinsweden.se

Studying in the USA

Fulbright Commission
www.fulbright.co.uk

EducationUSA
www.educationusa.info

College Board
www.collegeboard.com

College Navigator
http://nces.ed.gov/collegenavigator

National Association of Credential Evaluation Services (NACES)
www.naces.org

Common Application
www.commonapp.org

Hobsons Virtual Events
www.hobsonsevents.com
US virtual student fairs

Scholarships and financial aid
Edupass
www.edupass.org/finaid/databases.phtml

International Education Financial Aid
www.iefa.org

International Scholarships
www.internationalscholarships.com

US Citizenship and Immigration Services
www.uscis.gov

Studying in Canada

Study in Canada
www.educationau-incanada.ca

Association of Universities and Colleges of Canada
www.aucc.ca

Canadian Information Centre for International Credentials
www.cicic.ca

Citizenship & Immigration Canada
www.cic.gc.ca/english/study/index.asp

Immigration Québec
www.immigration-quebec.gouv.qc.ca/en

Statistics Canada
www.statcan.gc.ca

International Scholarships
www.scholarships-bourses.gc.ca/scholarships-bourses/index.
aspx?view=d
www.cbie.ca/english/scholarship/non_canadians.htm
www.acu.ac.uk/study_in_the_commonwealth/study
www.ScholarshipsCanada.com

Studying in Australia

Study in Australia
www.studyinaustralia.gov.au
www.study-in-australia.org/uk

Australian Qualifications Framework
www.aqf.edu.au

Australian Good University Guide
www.gooduniguide.com.au

Australian Educational International, National Office of Overseas
Skills Recognition (AEI NOOSR)
www.aei.gov.au/Services-And-Resources/Pages/AEINOOSR.aspx

Australian High Commission in London
www.uk.embassy.gov.au

Deptartment of Immigration & Citizenship
www.immi.gov.au

International Scholarships
www.acu.ac.uk/study_in_the_commonwealth/study
www.australiaawards.gov.au
www.britain-australia.org.uk/affiliations/northcotetrust.html

Finances and budgeting
www.moneysmart.gov.au/managing-my-money

Australian Tax Office
www.ato.gov.au

Studying in New Zealand

New Zealand Educated
www.newzealandeducated.com

New Zealand Qualifications Authority
www.nzqa.govt.nz/search

Fulbright Commission (Study in NZ)
www.fulbright.org.nz

Universities New Zealand
www.universitiesnz.ac.nz

Immigration New Zealand
www.immigration.govt.nz

New Zealand High Commission in London
www.nzembassy.com/united-kingdom

Student Job Search
www.sjs.co.nz

Inland Revenue Department
www.ird.govt.nz/how-to/irdnumbers

Studying in the rest of the world

Hong Kong
Study in Hong Kong
http://studyinhongkong.edu.hk/eng

Hong Kong Immigration Department
www.immd.gov.hk

South Africa
International Education Association of South Africa
www.studysa.co.za

South African Matriculation Board
www.hesa-enrol.ac.za/mb/forpres.htm

South African High Commission in London
http://southafricahouseuk.com

Malaysia
Study Malaysia
www.studymalaysia.com

Malaysian High Commission in London
www.kln.gov.my/perwakilan/london

Singapore
Singapore Education
www.singaporeedu.gov.sg

Contact Singapore
www.contactsingapore.sg

Ministry of Education website
www.moe.gov.sg

Immigration and Checkpoints Authority
www.ica.gov.sg

High Commission for the Republic of Singapore in London
www.mfa.gov.sg/london

Ministry of Manpower
www.mom.gov.sg

The Caribbean
Jamaica High Commission in London
www.jhcuk.org/citizens/universities

Caribbean Area Network for Quality Assurance in Tertiary
Education (CANQATE)
www.canqate.org/Links/RelatedLinks.aspx

China
China's University and College Admission System
www.cucas.edu.cn

Chinese Ministry of Education
www.moe.edu.cn

China Scholarship Council
www.csc.edu.cn

Chinese Embassy
www.visaforchina.org

Saudi Arabia

Ministry of Higher Education

www.mohe.gov.sa

Ministry of Foreign Affairs

www.mofa.gov.sa

Royal Embassy of Saudi Arabia in London

www.saudiembassy.org.uk

Qatar

Qatar Foundation for Education, Science and Community
Development www.qf.org.qa/education/universities

Japan

Study in Japan

www.studyjapan.go.jp/en

JUMP (Japanese Universities for Motivated People)

www.uni.international.mext.go.jp/global30

JASSO (Japan Student Services Organisation)

www.jasso.go.jp

Embassy of Japan in the UK

www.uk.emb-japan.go.jp

Utrecht University

 Universiteit Utrecht

Founded in 1636 and located in the heart of the Netherlands, Utrecht University is one of Europe's leading institutions for teaching and research. The university is engaged in high-quality and innovative research and collaborates with universities and research centres all over the world. Utrecht University provides an interdisciplinary environment and offers its students a personalised educational experience. A master's degree from our university gives you an edge if you want to do a PhD at Utrecht or get into another world-class university.

Our academic staff

You will be taught by dedicated experts – top researchers or professionals who also hold influential positions outside the university. Utrecht University academics want to get to know their students and build a relationship with them.

International environment

Each year, more than 2,000 international students come to Utrecht University to take part in its excellent English-language programmes and courses. They follow their ambition. Just like Utrecht University. We are proud to offer you a curriculum with an international perspective that educates and prepares you for an increasingly globalised world.

Master's programmes

Our one- and two-year English-taught master's degree programmes enable you to specialise in a specific area of interest to you. The programmes are designed to prepare you for a professional or research career.

Individual programme entry requirements may differ. Please check our website, www.uu.nl/internationalstudents.

Windesheim Honours College (WHC)

High-quality education in English

Do you want to study in Holland and study in English? Are you interested in creating a more sustainable world? Have you always dreamed of studying and working in an international atmosphere?

Windesheim Honours College (WHC) offers a Bachelor of Business Administration (BBA) degree with a specialisation in either Communication and Media or Public Health. Windesheim Honours College is a public university, therefore EU students pay home stay fees. We offer an intensive four-year programme with highly qualified and experienced staff from all over the world.

This unique programme combines traditional BBA subjects with a specialisation, and focusses on People, Planet and Profit. For more information about the curriculum check the website, www.windesheimhonourscollege.nl. The aim of the programme is to become a project manager, by bringing different stakeholders together to manage a project. This can be at governmental, NGO or corporate level. The programme is set up to provide students not only with a chance to learn the theory but also to put it into practice. Internships in semester five and eight ensure the students get international work experience during their studies. In addition, students can spend two semesters at a partner university where they can select electives. This way, they can specialise even further in their chosen field of expertise.

While at Windesheim Honours College students will be part of an international learning community, they stay at the residence and have classes together. Housing for all international students is guaranteed. We pride ourselves on personal contact between staff, lecturers and students.

Do you want to find out more about us? Visit our website or email us at honourscollege@windesheim.nl.

Roosevelt Academy

Roosevelt Academy

University College Roosevelt Academy (RA) is a small-scale international liberal arts and sciences college based in Middelburg in the southwest of the Netherlands. After three years of full-time studies, students receive their Bachelor of Arts (BA) or Bachelor of Science (BSc) degree from the renowned Utrecht University. Among the special characteristics of the academy are:

- English as the official language, both in class and on campus at large
- small-scale classes (with no more than 25 students)
- highly interactive and intensive method of instruction
- residential college with inner-city campus
- international staff and faculty.

RA's tight-knit academic community provides an environment that encourages intellectual exchange between students and professors in a friendly and informal atmosphere. The educational philosophy is based on the idea that a student benefits most from learning more about a variety of disciplines. This means that RA students put together their own programme with courses offered by the academy's four departments: academic core, arts and humanities, social sciences and science.

Courses offered range from a wide variety of disciplines, including anthropology, antiquity, chemistry, economics, French, German, geography, history, international law, life sciences, linguistics, mathematics, music and drama, philosophy, physics, political science, psychology, rhetoric, sociology, Spanish, and many more.

The tuition fee at RA is set by the Dutch government each year. For the year 2012–2013, students pay €2,271 in tuition fees (about £1,600). A full year of studying and living at RA is estimated to cost €10,000 (about £8,500).

For more information, see www.roac.nl.

Glossary

Academic transcript

A record of academic progress from around Y10 (Y11, NI and S3, Scotland) onwards, including exam results, unit grades, internal assessments, academic honours and explanations for any anomalies.

American College Test (ACT)

The ACT is used to determine academic potential for undergraduate study.

Associate degree

A two-year programme of higher education, often in a vocational subject such as hospitality or health.

Bologna process

A system to make higher education comparable and compatible across the EHEA, through use of mutually recognised systems and a clear credit framework.

Community college (USA)

These colleges offer two-year associate degrees, with the possibility of transferring to a university to top-up to a full degree; a cheaper option than going straight to a US university.

Core

The compulsory foundation for university study (used in North America and a number of other countries); students choose from a broad range of subjects.

Diploma mobility

Taking an entire degree overseas, as opposed to a study abroad or exchange programme.

Diploma supplement

A detailed transcript of attainment in higher education, recognised across the EHEA and beyond.

eCoE (electronic confirmation of enrolment)

The eCoE is issued by Australian colleges and universities as proof of enrolment and is required to apply for a student visa.

ECTS

European Credit Transfer and Accumulation System, aiding the transfer of students between institutions.

EHEA

European Higher Education Area; the countries where the Bologna process is utilised.

Elective

An optional course taken at university.

English medium

Education with English as the language of instruction.

Europass

Helps people to study, work or train across Europe, by presenting skills and qualifications in a standardised format that is easily understood in a range of countries.

Freshman year
First year (USA).

Junior year
Third year (USA).

Letter of intent
A statement demonstrating why you should be considered for your chosen course. The statement is used by the universities to distinguish between applicants. It may also be described as a letter of motivation, a statement of purpose or a personal statement.

Letter of motivation
A statement demonstrating why you should be considered for your chosen course, used by the universities to distinguish between applicants. It may also be described as a letter of intent, a statement of purpose or a personal statement.

Letter of recommendation
Reference letter to a potential university, most often (but not always) from a member of academic staff who can comment on your ability and potential.

Major
Your main subject area, for example history, engineering or nursing.

Midterm
An exam taken midway through the academic term.

Minor
A secondary subject area or a specialism of your major.

Numerus clausus (Germany)
A competitive system for courses that have more applicants than places.

Numerus fixus (Netherlands)
A fixed number of places are available on a course.

OECD
Organisation for Economic Co-operation and Development.

Orientation
Events and activities for new students, like freshers' week in the UK.

Polytechnic (New Zealand; Finland)
An institution providing professional or work-related higher education, in conjunction with business and industry; also known as a university of applied sciences.

Research-intensive or research-based university
An institution involved in extensive research activity and doctoral education.

Research proposal or research statement
The outline of an applicant's plans for research, including area of interest and rationale.

Scholastic Assessment Test (SAT)
Scholastic Assessment Test; used to determine academic potential for undergraduate study.

Semester
The two periods into which the academic year is divided in some countries.

Senior year
Fourth year (US).

Sophomore year
Second year (US).

Statement of purpose
A statement demonstrating why you should be considered for your chosen course. The statement is used by the universities to distinguish between applicants. It may also be described as a letter of intent, a letter of motivation or a personal statement.

Study abroad programme
A term often used to describe an exchange programme or short-term overseas study.

Tertiary education
Education following secondary level; it includes university education, as well as other post-18 education such as vocational training.

UNESCO
United Nations Educational, Scientific and Cultural Organisation.

University college (Denmark, Norway and Sweden)
An institution providing professional undergraduate degrees in areas like engineering, teaching or business.

University of applied sciences (Finland and the Netherlands)
See Polytechnic.

wānanga
An educational establishment in New Zealand that teaches degree-level courses in a Māori cultural context.

LEARN ALL THE ESSENTIALS

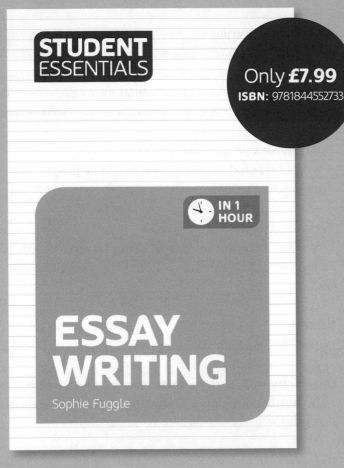

STUDENT ESSENTIALS

Only **£7.99**
ISBN: 9781844552733

IN 1 HOUR

ESSAY WRITING

Sophie Fuggle

Including how to:

✓ Plan your essay
✓ Develop a balanced argument
✓ Write a strong conclusion

Available to buy at

amazon.co.uk

trotman | **t**
www.trotman.co.uk

LEARN ALL THE ESSENTIALS

STUDENT ESSENTIALS

Only **£7.99**
ISBN: 9781844554171

IN 1 HOUR

STUDY SKILLS

Matt Potter

Including how to:

✓ Prepare for lectures
✓ Develop presentation skills
✓ Improve time management

Available to buy at

amazon.co.uk

trotman t
www.trotman.co.uk

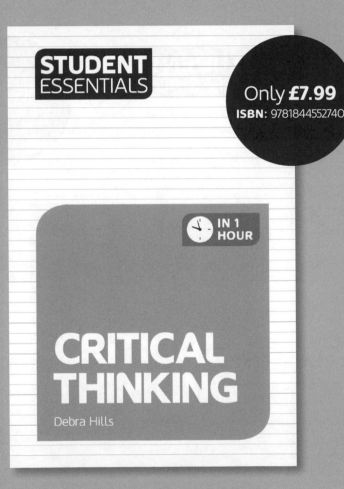

LEARN ALL THE ESSENTIALS

STUDENT ESSENTIALS

Only **£7.99**
ISBN: 9781844552740

IN 1 HOUR

CRITICAL THINKING

Debra Hills

Including how to:
- ✓ Build arguments
- ✓ Use analytical techniques
- ✓ Create comprehensive arguments

Available to buy at

amazon.co.uk

trotman t

www.trotman.co.uk